Crochet

for the home

LEISURE ARTS, INC. • Maumelle, Arkansas

Contents

Simple Crochet Math

Yarn = Inspiration
Hooks = Creation
Yarn + Hooks = Happiness

Who doesn't love to fill their homes with beautiful and useful items? We've filled this book with 40 lovely and easy to crochet projects for you to decorate your home or give as gifts.

Starting with the most essential rooms in the house, the kitchen & bath: make a set of ripple placemats in fresh white & teal tones, throw a splash of color on the table with bright coasters, whip up a batch of dishcloths (there are 4 to choose from) or crochet a face cloth with matching face scrubbie and bath pouf.

Don't sacrifice style for comfort or vice versa; choose from an assortment of cozy afghans, trendy pillows & plush rugs to accent your home. There's even a giant pouf for you to put your feet up at the end of a long day! Your furry companions will love the pet bed & blanket designs, too.

Everyone needs more storage; we've got 5 cute baskets to help out. And finally, have some fun with a funky, textured wall hanging, colorful mandala & a mini banner that also looks great tied on a purse or tote bag.

Change the colors to suit your style & décor. Each project is easy to make with our step-by-step instructions. Most use medium weight yarn; a few use bulky or super bulky weight yarn, so they will come together in a flash.

for the kitchen and bath

Ripple Placemat

EASY

Finished Size: 11½" x 17½" (29 cm x 44.5 cm)

SHOPPING LIST

Yarn (Medium Weight) 4

[4.5 ounces, 247 yards (127 grams, 225 meters) per skein]:

- ☐ White - 150 yards (137 meters)
- ☐ Gray - 40 yards (36.5 meters)
- ☐ Green - 40 yards (36.5 meters)

Note: Yarn amounts are for one Placemat.

Crochet Hook

- ☐ Size I (5.5 mm) **or size needed for gauge**

GAUGE INFORMATION

In pattern, one point to point repeat (11 sts) = 2¼" (5.75 cm); 9 rows = 3" (7.5 cm)

Gauge Swatch: 4½" wide x 3¼" high (11.5 cm x 8.25 cm)

Ch 24.

Work same as Placemat through Row 9: 15 sc and 8 ch-1 sps.

PLACEMAT

With White, ch 57.

Row 1 (Right side)**:** Working in back ridges of beginning ch ***(Fig. 2, page 124)***, 2 sc in second ch from hook, (ch 1, skip next ch, sc in next ch) twice, skip next 2 chs, (sc in next ch, ch 1, skip next ch) twice, ★ 3 sc in next ch, (ch 1, skip next ch, sc in next ch) twice, skip next 2 chs, (sc in next ch, ch 1, skip next ch) twice; repeat from ★ across to last ch, 2 sc in last ch: 36 sc and 20 ch-1 sps.

Note: Loop a short piece of yarn around any stitch to mark Row 1 as **right** side.

Rows 2-4: Ch 1, turn; 2 sc in first sc, ch 1, sc in next ch-1 sp, ch 1, sc in next 2 ch-1 sps, ch 1, sc in next ch-1 sp, ch 1, ★ skip next sc, 3 sc in next sc, ch 1, sc in next ch-1 sp, ch 1, sc in next 2 ch-1 sps, ch 1, sc in next ch-1 sp, ch 1; repeat from ★ across to last 2 sc, skip next sc, 2 sc in last sc; at end of Row 4, finish off.

Row 5: With **right** side facing, join Gray with sc in first sc ***(see Joining With Sc, page 123)***; sc in same st, ch 1, sc in next ch-1 sp, ch 1, sc in next 2 ch-1 sps, ch 1, sc in next ch-1 sp, ch 1, ★ skip next sc, 3 sc in next sc, ch 1, sc in next ch-1 sp, ch 1, sc in next 2 ch-1 sps, ch 1, sc in next ch-1 sp, ch 1; repeat from ★ across to last 2 sc, skip next sc, 2 sc in last sc; finish off.

Row 6: With **wrong** side facing, join Green with sc in first sc; sc in same st, ch 1, sc in next ch-1 sp, ch 1, sc in next 2 ch-1 sps, ch 1, sc in next ch-1 sp, ch 1, ★ skip next sc, 3 sc in next sc, ch 1, sc in next ch-1 sp, ch 1, sc in next 2 ch-1 sps, ch 1, sc in next ch-1 sp, ch 1; repeat from ★ across to last 2 sc, skip next sc, 2 sc in last sc; finish off.

Row 7: With **right** side facing, join Gray with sc in first sc; sc in same st, ch 1, sc in next ch-1 sp, ch 1, sc in next 2 ch-1 sps, ch 1, sc in next ch-1 sp, ch 1, ★ skip next sc, 3 sc in next sc, ch 1, sc in next ch-1 sp, ch 1, sc in next 2 ch-1 sps, ch 1, sc in next ch-1 sp, ch 1; repeat from ★ across to last 2 sc, skip next sc, 2 sc in last sc; finish off.

Row 8: With **wrong** side facing, join White with sc in first sc; sc in same st, ch 1, sc in next ch-1 sp, ch 1, sc in next 2 ch-1 sps, ch 1, sc in next ch-1 sp, ch 1, ★ skip next sc, 3 sc in next sc, ch 1, sc in next ch-1 sp, ch 1, sc in next 2 ch-1 sps, ch 1, sc in next ch-1 sp, ch 1; repeat from ★ across to last 2 sc, skip next sc, 2 sc in last sc; do **not** finish off.

Rows 9-11: Ch 1, turn; 2 sc in first sc, ch 1, sc in next ch-1 sp, ch 1, sc in next 2 ch-1 sps, ch 1, sc in next ch-1 sp, ch 1, ★ skip next sc, 3 sc in next sc, ch 1, sc in next ch-1 sp, ch 1, sc in next 2 ch-1 sps, ch 1, sc in next ch-1 sp, ch 1; repeat from ★ across to last 2 sc, skip next sc, 2 sc in last sc; at end of Row 11, finish off.

Row 12: With **wrong** side facing, join Green with sc in first sc; sc in same st, ch 1, sc in next ch-1 sp, ch 1, sc in next 2 ch-1 sps, ch 1, sc in next ch-1 sp, ch 1, ★ skip next sc, 3 sc in next sc, ch 1, sc in next ch-1 sp, ch 1, sc in next 2 ch-1 sps, ch 1, sc in next ch-1 sp, ch 1; repeat from ★ across to last 2 sc, skip next sc, 2 sc in last sc; finish off.

Row 13: With **right** side facing, join Gray with sc in first sc; sc in same st, ch 1, sc in next ch-1 sp, ch 1, sc in next 2 ch-1 sps, ch 1, sc in next ch-1 sp, ch 1, ★ skip next sc, 3 sc in next sc, ch 1, sc in next ch-1 sp, ch 1, sc in next 2 ch-1 sps, ch 1, sc in next ch-1 sp, ch 1; repeat from ★ across to last 2 sc, skip next sc, 2 sc in last sc; finish off.

Row 14: With **wrong** side facing, join Green with sc in first sc; sc in same st, ch 1, sc in next ch-1 sp, ch 1, sc in next 2 ch-1 sps, ch 1, sc in next ch-1 sp, ch 1, ★ skip next sc, 3 sc in next sc, ch 1, sc in next ch-1 sp, ch 1, sc in next 2 ch-1 sps, ch 1, sc in next ch-1 sp, ch 1; repeat from ★ across to last 2 sc, skip next sc, 2 sc in last sc; finish off.

Row 15: With **right** side facing, join White with sc in first sc; sc in same st, ch 1, sc in next ch-1 sp, ch 1, sc in next 2 ch-1 sps, ch 1, sc in next ch-1 sp, ch 1, ★ skip next sc, 3 sc in next sc, ch 1, sc in next ch-1 sp, ch 1, sc in next 2 ch-1 sps, ch 1, sc in next ch-1 sp, ch 1; repeat from ★ across to last 2 sc, skip next sc, 2 sc in last sc; do **not** finish off.

Rows 16-18: Ch 1, turn; 2 sc in first sc, ch 1, sc in next ch-1 sp, ch 1, sc in next 2 ch-1 sps, ch 1, sc in next ch-1 sp, ch 1, ★ skip next sc, 3 sc in next sc, ch 1, sc in next ch-1 sp, ch 1, sc in next 2 ch-1 sps, ch 1, sc in next ch-1 sp, ch 1; repeat from ★ across to last 2 sc, skip next sc, 2 sc in last sc; at end of Row 18, finish off.

Rows 19-53: Repeat Rows 5-18 twice; then repeat Rows 5-11 once **more**.

Design by Kathleen Stuart.

Dishcloth Trio

EASY

Finished Size: Approximately 10" (25.5 cm) square

SHOPPING LIST

Yarn (Medium Weight Cotton) MEDIUM 4
[2.75 ounces, 94 yards (78 grams, 86 meters) per skein]:

- ☐ Print - 1 skein **each** dishcloth

[3 ounces, 103 yards (85 grams, 94 meters) per skein]:

- ☐ Solid - 1 skein **each** dishcloth

Crochet Hook

- ☐ Size K (6.5 mm)

GAUGE INFORMATION

Gauge is not important. Your dishcloths can be slightly larger or smaller without changing the overall effect.

STITCH GUIDE

FOUNDATION SINGLE CROCHET ***(abbreviated foundation sc)***

To begin, ch 2, insert hook in second ch from hook, YO and pull up a loop, YO and draw through one loop on hook **(ch 1 made)**, YO and draw through both loops on hook **(first foundation sc made)**.

To work each additional foundation sc, insert hook in ch at base of sc just made, YO and pull up a loop, YO and draw through one loop on hook **(ch 1 made)**, YO and draw through both loops on hook **(foundation sc made, *Fig. A*)**.

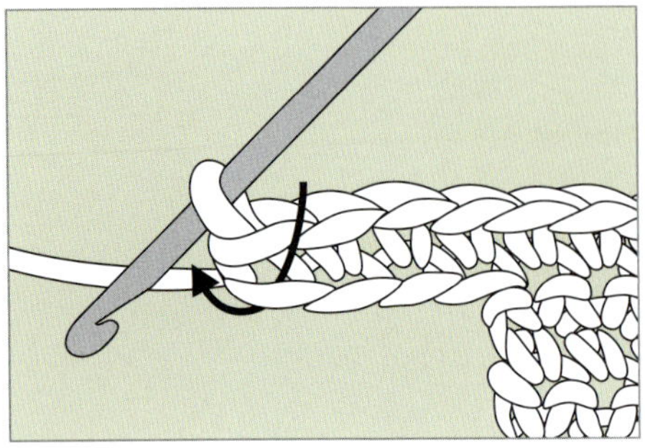

Fig. A

TREBLE CROCHET ***(abbreviated tr)***

YO twice, insert hook in st indicated, YO and pull up a loop (4 loops on hook), (YO and draw through 2 loops on hook) 3 times.

FRONT POST TREBLE CROCHET ***(abbreviated FPtr)***

YO twice, insert hook from **front** to **back** around post of st indicated ***(Fig. 6, page 124)***, YO and pull up a loop (4 loops on hook), (YO and draw through 2 loops on hook) 3 times.

BACK POST TREBLE CROCHET ***(abbreviated BPtr)***

YO twice, insert hook from **back** to **front** around post of st indicated ***(Fig. 6, page 124)***, YO and pull up a loop (4 loops on hook), (YO and draw through 2 loops on hook) 3 times.

1. Slanting Wedge Stitch

Row 1: Work 30 foundation sc.

Row 2: Ch 1, turn; (hdc, dc) in first st, ★ skip next 2 sts, (sc, hdc, dc) in next st; repeat from ★ across to last 2 sts, skip last 2 sts, sc in turning ch.

Repeat Row 2 for pattern until all the yarn is used **or** Dishcloth is desired size.

Finish off.

2. Offset Knot Stitch

Row 1 (Right side)**:** Work 29 foundation sc.

Row 2: Ch 1, turn; sc in first sc, (tr in next sc, sc in next sc pushing tr to the **back**) across.

Row 3: Ch 1, turn; sc in each st across.

Row 4: Ch 1, turn; tr in first sc, (sc in next sc pushing tr to the **back**, tr in next sc) across to last 2 sc, sc in last 2 sc pushing tr to the **back**.

Row 5: Ch 1, turn; sc in each st across.

Repeat Rows 2-5 for pattern until all the yarn is used **or** Dishcloth is desired size, ending by working Row 3 or Row 5.

Finish off.

2

3. Staggered Post Stitch

Ch 33.

Row 1: Tr in fourth ch from hook and in each ch across: 31 sts.

Row 2: Ch 4 **(counts as first tr, now and throughout)**, turn; (work FPtr around next st, work BPtr around next st) across.

Rows 3-5: Repeat Row 2, 3 times.

Row 6: Ch 2 **(counts as first hdc, now and throughout)**, turn; hdc in next st and in each st across.

Rows 7-12: Ch 2, turn; hdc in first hdc, (skip next hdc, 2 hdc in next hdc) across to last 2 hdc, skip next hdc, hdc in last hdc.

Row 13: Ch 2, turn; hdc in next hdc and in each hdc across.

What better place for texture than in the kitchen? This trio is easy to make and great to use!

Row 14: Ch 4, turn; tr in next hdc and in each hdc across.

Rows 15-18: Repeat Row 2, 4 times.

Finish off.

Designs by Sheryl Means.

Tablerunner

EASY

Finished Size: 24" wide x 48" long (61 cm x 122 cm)

SHOPPING LIST

Yarn (Fine Weight) FINE 2

[3.5 ounces, 317 yards (100 grams, 290 meters) per ball]:

- ☐ Gray - 2 balls
- ☐ Turquoise - 2 balls
- ☐ Cream - 2 balls

Crochet Hook

- ☐ Size F (3.75 mm) **or** size needed for gauge

Additional Supplies

- ☐ Tapestry needle

GAUGE INFORMATION

Gauge Swatch: 3" (7.5 cm) square
Work same as Square on page 20 through Rnd 3: 48 dc.

STITCH GUIDE

CLUSTER (uses next 3 dc)
★ YO, insert hook in **next** dc, YO and pull up a loop, YO and draw through 2 loops on hook; repeat from ★ 2 times **more**, YO and draw through all 4 loops on hook.

PICOT
Ch 3, slip st in top of last sc made.

SINGLE CROCHET 2 TOGETHER *(abbreviated sc2tog)*
Pull up a loop in same sp and in next sp, YO and draw through all 3 loops on hook (counts as one sc).

SQUARE

(Make 6 **each** of 3 colors)

Ch 12; join with slip st to form a ring.

Rnd 1 (Right side)**:** Ch 3 **(counts as first dc, now and throughout)**, 6 dc in ring, (ch 3, 7 dc in ring) 3 times, ch 1, hdc in first dc to form last ch-3 sp: 28 dc.

Note: Loop a short piece of yarn around any stitch to mark Rnd 1 as **right** side.

Rnd 2: Ch 3, dc in last ch-3 sp made and in next dc, ch 5, skip next 5 dc, dc in next dc, ★ (2 dc, ch 3, 2 dc) in next ch-3 sp, dc in next dc, ch 5, skip next 5 dc, dc in next dc; repeat from ★ 2 times **more**, 2 dc in same sp as first dc, ch 1, hdc in first dc to form last ch-3 sp: 24 dc.

Rnd 3: Ch 3, 2 dc in last ch-3 sp made, dc in next 3 dc, ch 3, sc in center ch of next ch-5, ch 3, dc in next 3 dc, ★ (3 dc, ch 3, 3 dc) in next ch-3 sp, dc in next 3 dc, ch 3, sc in center ch of next ch-5, ch 3, dc in next 3 dc; repeat from ★ 2 times **more**, 3 dc in same sp as first dc, ch 1, hdc in first dc to form last ch-3 sp: 48 dc.

Rnd 4: Ch 3, 2 dc in last ch-3 sp made, dc in next 6 dc, ch 5, skip next 2 ch-3 sps, dc in next 6 dc, ★ (3 dc, ch 3, 3 dc) in next ch-3 sp, dc in next 6 dc, ch 5, skip next 2 ch-3 sps, dc in next 6 dc; repeat from ★ 2 times **more**, 3 dc in same sp as first dc, ch 1, hdc in first dc to form last ch-3 sp: 72 dc.

Rnd 5: Ch 3, 2 dc in last ch-3 sp made, dc in next 9 dc, ch 3, sc in center ch of next ch-5, ch 3, dc in next 9 dc, ★ (3 dc, ch 3, 3 dc) in next ch-3 sp, dc in next 9 dc, ch 3, sc in center ch of next ch-5, ch 3, dc in next 9 dc; repeat from ★ 2 times **more**, 3 dc in same sp as first dc, ch 1, hdc in first dc to form last ch-3 sp: 96 dc.

Rnd 6: Ch 3, 2 dc in last ch-3 sp made, dc in next 12 dc, ch 5, skip next 2 ch-3 sps, dc in next 12 dc, ★ (3 dc, ch 3, 3 dc) in next ch-3 sp, dc in next 12 dc, ch 5, skip next 2 ch-3 sps, dc in next 12 dc; repeat from ★ 2 times **more**, 3 dc in same sp as first dc, ch 1, hdc in first dc to form last ch-3 sp: 120 dc.

Rnd 7: Ch 3, 2 dc in last ch-3 sp made, dc in next 15 dc, ch 3, sc in center ch of next ch-5, ch 3, dc in next 15 dc, ★ (3 dc, ch 3, 3 dc) in next ch-3 sp, dc in next 15 dc, ch 3, sc in center ch of next ch-5, ch 3, dc in next 15 dc; repeat from ★ 2 times **more**, 3 dc in same sp as first dc, ch 1, hdc in first dc to form last ch-3 sp: 144 dc.

Rnd 8: Ch 3, 2 dc in last ch-3 sp made, ch 5, (skip next 3 dc, work Cluster, ch 5) 3 times, skip next 2 ch-3 sps, (work Cluster, ch 5, skip next 3 dc) 3 times, ★ (3 dc, ch 3, 3 dc) in next ch-3 sp, ch 5, (skip next 3 dc, work Cluster, ch 5) 3 times, skip next 2 ch-3 sps, (work Cluster, ch 5, skip next 3 dc) 3 times; repeat from ★ 2 times **more**, 3 dc in same sp as first dc, ch 1, hdc in first dc to form last ch-3 sp: 24 Clusters.

Rnd 9: Ch 3, 2 dc in last ch-3 sp made, 6 sc in each of next 3 ch-5 sps, (3 sc, ch 3, slip st in top of last sc made, 3 sc) in next ch-5 sp, 6 sc in each of next 3 ch-5 sps, ★ (3 dc, ch 3, 3 dc) in next ch-3 sp, 6 sc in each of next 3 ch-5 sps, (3 sc, ch 3, slip st in top of last sc made, 3 sc) in next ch-5 sp, 6 sc in each of next 3 ch-5 sps; repeat from ★ 2 times **more**, 3 dc in same sp as first dc, ch 3; join with slip st to first dc, finish off leaving a long end for sewing.

ASSEMBLY

Using photo as a guide for placement, having **wrong** sides together and working through **both** loops on **both** pieces, whipstitch squares together with long ends ***(Fig. 12a, page 126)***, forming 3 strips of 6 squares **each**; then whipstitch strips together in same manner.

EDGING

With **right** side facing, join Gray with sc in any corner ch-3 sp ***(see Joining With Sc, page 123)***; (2 sc, work Picot, 2 sc) in same sp, sc in next 12 sts, ★ † (work Picot, sc in next 12 sts) 3 times, ♥ sc in next sp, sc2tog, work Picot, sc in same sp and in next 12 sts, (work Picot, sc in next 12 sts) 3 times ♥; repeat from ♥ to ♥ across to next corner ch-3 sp †, (3 sc, work Picot, 2 sc) in corner sp, sc in next 12 sts; repeat from ★ 2 times **more**, then repeat from † to † once; join with slip st to first sc, finish off.

Design by Shobha Govindan.

Dishcloth & Dishtowel

EASY

Finished Sizes:
Dishcloth - 9½" (24 cm) square
Dishtowel - 15¼" wide x 18½" high (38.5 cm x 47 cm)

SHOPPING LIST

Yarn (Medium Weight) MEDIUM 4
[2.5 ounces, 120 yards (70.9 grams, 109 meters) per skein]:
- ☐ 3 skeins

Crochet Hook
- ☐ Size H (5 mm) **or** size needed for gauge

Additional Supplies
(For Dishtowel only)
- ☐ Button
- ☐ Sewing needle and thread

GAUGE INFORMATION

In pattern,
8 sps and 12 rows = 3¾" (9.5 cm)
Gauge Swatch: 3¾" (9.5 cm) square
Ch 18.
Rows 1-12: Work same as Dishcloth: 8 sps.
Finish off.

Dishcloth

Ch 42.

Row 1: Sc in fourth ch from hook, ★ ch 1, skip next ch, sc in next ch; repeat from ★ across: 20 sps.

Row 2: Ch 3, turn; sc in first ch-1 sp, (ch 1, sc in next sp) across.

Repeat Row 2 for pattern until piece measures 9" (23 cm) from beginning ch, working an even number of rows.

Edging: Ch 1, turn; (sc, ch 3, sc) in first ch-1 sp, ch 1, (sc in next ch-1 sp, ch 1) across to last ch-3 sp, (sc, ch 3, sc) in last ch-3 sp, ch 1; working in ends of rows, skip first 2 rows, † sc in next row, ch 1, skip next row †; repeat from † to † across; working in sps across beginning ch, (sc, ch 3, sc) in first sp, ch 1, (sc in next sp, ch 1) across to last sp, (sc, ch 3, sc) in last sp, ch 1; working in ends of rows, skip first 2 rows, repeat from † to † across; join with slip st to first sc, finish off.

Dishtowel

BODY

Ch 66.

Row 1 (Right side)**:** Sc in second ch from hook and in each ch across: 65 sc.

Note: Loop a short piece of yarn around any stitch to mark Row 1 as **right** side.

Row 2: Ch 1, turn; sc in first sc, ★ ch 1, skip next sc, sc in next sc; repeat from ★ across: 33 sc and 32 ch-1 sps.

Row 3: Ch 1, turn; sc in each sc and in each ch-1 sp across: 65 sc.

Repeat Rows 2 and 3 for pattern until piece measures approximately 13" (33 cm) from beginning ch, ending by working Row 3.

SHAPING

Row 1: Ch 3 **(counts as first dc, now and throughout)**, turn; dc in next sc and in each sc across.

Row 2 (Decrease row)**:** Ch 3, turn; (skip next dc, dc in next dc) across: 33 dc.

Row 3: Ch 3, turn; dc in next dc and in each dc across.

Rows 4-8: Repeat Rows 2 and 3 twice, then repeat Row 2 once **more**: 5 dc.

Rows 9-17: Ch 3, turn; dc in next dc and in each dc across.

Row 18: Ch 3, turn; dc in next dc, ch 1, skip next dc **(buttonhole made)**, dc in last 2 dc: 4 dc and one ch-1 sp.

Row 19: Ch 3, turn; dc in next dc and in next ch-1 sp, dc in last 2 dc; finish off.

With **right** side facing, sew button to center dc on Row 5 of Shaping.

Designs by Roberta Maier.

Bright Coaster Set

EASY

Finished Size: 4" (10 cm) square

SHOPPING LIST

Yarn (Medium Weight Cotton) MEDIUM 4
[2.5 ounces, 120 yards
(70.9 grams, 109 meters) per ball]:

- ☐ Yellow - 25 yards (23 meters)
- ☐ Pink - 25 yards (23 meters)
- ☐ Orange - 25 yards (23 meters)
- ☐ Green - 25 yards (23 meters)

Crochet Hook

- ☐ Size H (5 mm)
  or size needed for gauge

GAUGE INFORMATION

15 sc = 4" (10 cm)
Gauge Swatch: 4" wide x 1¼" high
(10 cm x 3.25 cm)
Work same as Coaster for 6 rows; do **not** finish off.

COASTER

Ch 16.

Row 1 (Wrong side)**:** Sc in back ridge of second ch from hook and each ch across *(Fig. 2, page 124)*: 15 sc.

Note: Loop a short piece of yarn around the **back** of any stitch on Row 1 as **right** side.

Row 2: Ch 1, turn; working in Back Loops Only of sc on Row 1 **and** in one free loop of beginning ch *(Fig. A)*, sc in each st across.

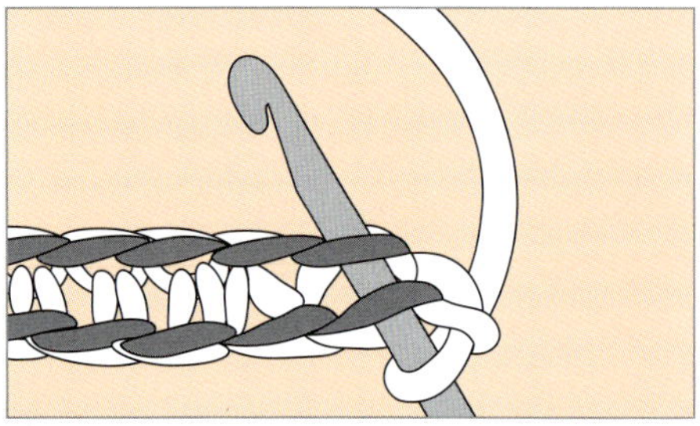

Fig. A

Rows 3-22: Ch 1, turn; working in Back Loops Only of sts on last row **and** in free loops of previous row *(Fig. B)*, sc in each st across.

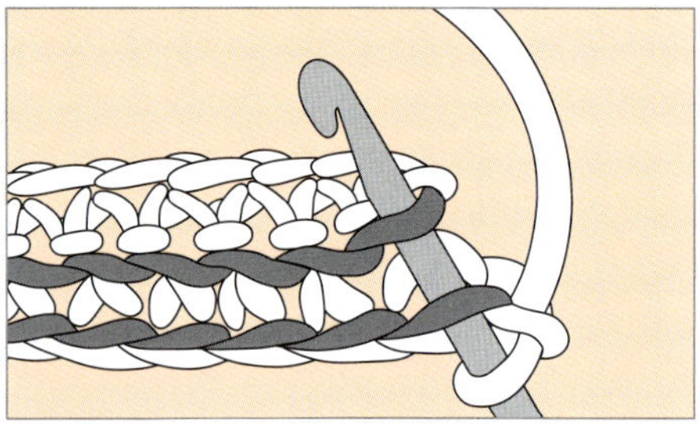

Fig. B

Row 23: Ch 1, turn; working in **both** loops of sts on Row 22 **and** in free loops of previous row, sc in each st across; finish off.

Bath Set

Face Cloth

EASY

Finished Size: 8" (20.5 cm) square

SHOPPING LIST

Yarn (Medium Weight) MEDIUM 4

☐ 75 yards (68.5 meters)

Crochet Hook

☐ Size J (6 mm)
or size needed for gauge

GAUGE INFORMATION

In pattern, 10 sts = 3" (7.5 cm)
Gauge Swatch: 7½" (19 cm) wide
Work same as Cloth for 4 rows: 25 sts.

BODY

Ch 26.

Row 1: (Sc, dc) in second ch from hook, ★ skip next ch, (sc, dc) in next ch; repeat from ★ across to last 2 chs, skip next ch, sc in last ch: 25 sts.

Row 2: Ch 1, turn; (sc, dc) in first sc, ★ skip next dc, (sc, dc) in next sc; repeat from ★ across to last 2 sts, skip next dc, sc in last sc.

Repeat Row 2 for pattern until Cloth measures approximately 7½" (19 cm) from beginning ch.

EDGING

Ch 1, do **not** turn; sc evenly around entire Cloth, working 3 sc in each corner ***(Fig. 5b, page 124)***; join with slip st to first sc, finish off.

Face Scrubbie

EASY

Finished Size: 4" (10 cm) diameter

SHOPPING LIST

Yarn (Medium Weight) MEDIUM 4

☐ Main Color - 15 yards (13.5 meters) **each**

☐ Contrasting Color - 10 yards (9 meters) **each**

Crochet Hook

☐ Size G (4 mm)
or size needed for gauge

GAUGE INFORMATION

Gauge Swatch: 2½" (6.25 cm) diameter
Work same as Scrubbie through Rnd 2 of Base: 28 dc.

BASE

Rnd 1 (Right side)**:** With Main Color, make an adjustable loop to form a ring ***(Figs. 1a-d, page 123)***; (sc, hdc, 12 dc) in ring; do **not** join, place marker to indicate beginning of rnd ***(see Markers, page 123)***: 14 sts.

Note: Loop a short piece of yarn around any stitch to mark Rnd 1 as **right** side.

Rnd 2: Working in Back Loops Only ***(Fig. 4, page 124)***, 2 dc in each st around: 28 dc.

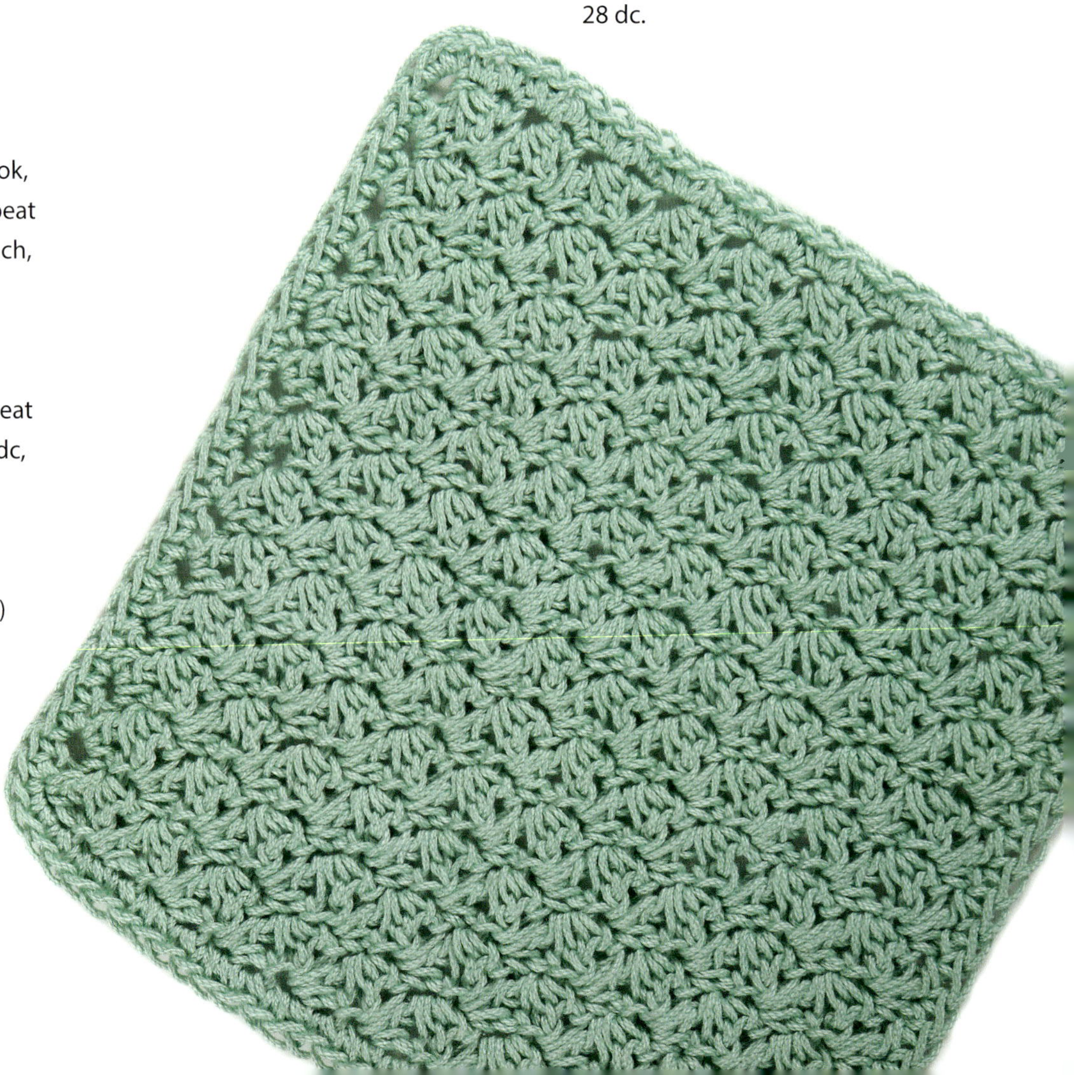

Rnd 3: Working in Back Loops Only, (dc in next dc, 2 dc in next dc) around to marker; remove marker, hdc in next dc, sc in next dc, slip st in next dc; finish off: 42 sts.

TRIM

With **right** side facing and working in free loops of Base ***(Fig. 5a, page 124)***, join Contrasting Color with slip st in first sc on Rnd 1; (ch 3, slip st) in each st around Base to slip st at end of Rnd 3; (ch 1, slip st) in both loops of each dc around; finish off.

Bath Pouf

EASY

Finished Size: Approximately 5" (12.5 cm) diameter

SHOPPING LIST

Yarn (Medium Weight) 4

- ☐ Main Color - 100 yards (91 meters) **each**
- ☐ Contrasting Color - 60 yards (55 meters) **each**

Crochet Hook

- ☐ Size I (5.5 mm)

GAUGE INFORMATION

Gauge is not important. Your Pouf can be slightly smaller or larger without changing the overall effect.

BASE

Rnd 1: With Main Color, make an adjustable ring ***(Figs. 1a-d, page 123)***; ch 40 for hanger, being careful **not** to twist ch, slip st in ring, ch 5 **(counts as first dc plus ch 2)**, (dc, ch 2) 14 times in ring; working in **front** of hanger, join with slip st to first dc: 15 ch-2 sps.

Rnds 2 and 3: Slip st in first ch-2 sp, ch 5, (dc, ch 2) 4 times in same sp, (dc, ch 2) 5 times in each ch-2 sp around; join with slip st to first dc.

Finish off.

TRIM

With same side facing, join Contrasting Color with sc in any ch-2 sp ***(see Joining With Sc, page 123)***; sc in next dc, (sc in next ch-2 sp, sc in next dc) around; join with slip st to first sc, finish off.

Flower Sachet

EASY

Finished Size: 4¾" (12 cm) diameter

SHOPPING LIST

Yarn (Lace Weight) LACE 0

- ☐ MC (Green) - 35 yards (32 meters)
- ☐ CC (Aqua) - 25 yards (23 meters)

Steel Crochet Hook

- ☐ Size 6 (1.8 mm) **or** size needed for gauge

Additional Supplies

- ☐ ¼" (6 mm) Ribbon - 24" (61 cm)
- ☐ Bridal net - 5" x 20" (12.5 cm x 51 cm)
- ☐ Sewing needle and thread
- ☐ Potpourri - approximately ½ ounce (14 grams)

GAUGE INFORMATION

Gauge Swatch: 2¾" (7 cm) diameter
Work same as Front through Rnd 4: 20 Petals:

STITCH GUIDE

TREBLE CROCHET ***(abbreviated tr)***
YO twice, insert hook in st indicated, YO and pull up a loop (4 loops on hook), (YO and draw through 2 loops on hook) 3 times.

CLUSTER (uses one st)
YO twice, insert hook in fourth ch from hook, YO and pull up a loop, (YO and draw through 2 loops on hook) twice, YO twice, insert hook in **same** ch, YO and pull up a loop, (YO and draw through 2 loops on hook) twice, YO and draw through all 3 loops on hook.

FRONT

Rnd 1 (Right side)**:** With CC, ch 6, (dc, ch 2) 9 times in sixth ch from hook **(5 skipped chs count as first dc plus ch 2)**; join with slip st to first dc: 10 dc and 10 ch-2 sps.

Note: Loop a short piece of yarn around any stitch to mark Rnd 1 as **right** side.

Rnd 2: (Slip st, ch 1, sc) in next ch-2 sp, (ch 3, sc in next ch-2 sp) around, ch 1, hdc in first sc to form last ch-3 sp.

Rnd 3: Ch 1, sc in last ch-3 sp made, ch 4, (sc in next ch-3 sp, ch 4) around; join with sip st to first first sc.

Rnd 4: (Slip st, ch 1, sc) in next ch-4 sp, [ch 7, hdc in second ch from hook, dc in next ch, tr in next 2 chs, dc in next ch, sc in next ch **(Petal made)**], sc in same ch-4 sp, work Petal, (sc, work Petal) twice in each ch-4 sp around; join with slip st to first sc, finish off: 20 Petals.

BORDER

Rnd 1: With **right** side facing and working in ch at tip of Petals, join MC with sc in any Petal ***(see Joining With Sc, page 123)***; ch 4, work Cluster, ★ sc in next Petal, ch 4, work Cluster; repeat from ★ around; join with slip st to first sc: 20 sc and 20 Clusters.

Rnd 2: Ch 8 **(counts as first dc plus ch 5)**, skip next Cluster, ★ dc in next sc, ch 5, skip next Cluster; repeat from ★ around; join with slip st to first dc: 20 dc and 20 ch-5 sps.

Rnd 3 (Eyelet rnd)**:** Ch 4 **(counts as first dc plus ch 1)**, skip next ch, (dc in next ch, ch 1, skip next ch) twice, ★ dc in next dc, ch 1, skip next ch, (dc in next ch, ch 1, skip next ch) twice; repeat from ★ around; join with slip st to first dc: 60 dc and 60 ch-1 sps.

Rnd 4: Ch 7 **(counts as first dc plus ch 4)**, work Cluster, skip next dc, ★ dc in next dc, ch 4, work Cluster, skip next dc; repeat from ★ around; join with slip st to first dc, finish off.

BACK

Work same as Front through Rnd 3 of Border; finish off.

FINISHING

Make a double-thick pouch as follows: Using Back for a pattern, cut four circles from bridal net for each pouch, allowing ¼" (6 mm) for seam allowance. Sew all pieces of net together, leaving a 2" (5 cm) opening. Turn seam to inside.

Fill with potpourri and stitch opening closed.

With ribbon, weave Front and Back together through Eyelet round, inserting pouch before closing.

Tie in a bow.

Design by Anne Halliday.

for comfort and style

Basketweave Runner

EASY

Finished Size: 26" x 57½" (66 cm x 146 cm)

SHOPPING LIST

Yarn (Super Bulky Weight) 6
[10.5 ounces, 220 yards (300 grams, 201 meters) per skein]:
☐ 4 skeins

Crochet Hook
☐ Size N/P (10 mm) **or** size needed for gauge

GAUGE INFORMATION

In pattern, 6 sts = 3½" (9 cm)
4 rows = 4" (10 cm)

Gauge Swatch: 4¾" wide x 4" high (12 cm x 10 cm)

Ch 9.

Rows 1-4: Work same as Rug: 8 sts.

Finish off.

STITCH GUIDE

FRONT POST HALF DOUBLE CROCHET *(abbreviated FPhdc)*

YO, insert hook from **front** to **back** around post of st indicated ***(Fig. 6, page 124)***, YO and pull up a loop, YO and draw through all 3 loops on hook.

BACK POST HALF DOUBLE CROCHET *(abbreviated BPhdc)*

YO, insert hook from **back** to **front** around post of st indicated ***(Fig. 6, page 124)***, YO and pull up a loop, YO and draw through all 3 loops on hook.

BODY

Ch 45, place marker in second ch from hook for st placement.

Row 1 (Right side)**:** Hdc in third ch from hook **(2 skipped chs count as first hdc)** and in each ch across: 44 hdc.

Row 2: Ch 2 **(counts as first hdc, now and throughout)**, turn; work FPhdc around each of next 2 hdc, ★ work BPhdc around each of next 2 hdc, work FPhdc around each of next 2 hdc; repeat from ★ across to last hdc, hdc in last hdc.

Row 3: Ch 2, turn; work BPhdc around each of next 2 sts, ★ work FPhdc around each of next 2 sts, work BPhdc around each of next 2 sts; repeat from ★ across to last hdc, hdc in last hdc.

Rows 4 and 5: Ch 2, turn; work FPhdc around each of next 2 sts, ★ work BPhdc around each of next 2 sts, work FPhdc around each of next 2 sts; repeat from ★ across to last hdc, hdc in last hdc.

Row 6: Ch 2, turn; work BPhdc around each of next 2 sts, ★ work FPhdc around each of next 2 sts, work BPhdc around each of next 2 sts; repeat from ★ across to last hdc, hdc in last hdc.

Rows 7 and 8: Ch 2, turn; work FPhdc around each of next 2 sts, ★ work BPhdc around each of next 2 sts, work FPhdc around each of next 2 sts; repeat from ★ across to last hdc, hdc in last hdc.

Repeat Rows 3-8 for pattern until piece measures approximately 57" (145 cm) from beginning ch, ending by working Row 7.

Edging: Ch 1, do **not** turn; sc evenly across ends of rows to beginning ch; working in free loops of beginning ch ***(Fig. 5b, page 124)***, 2 sc in first ch, sc in each ch across to marked ch, 2 sc in marked ch, remove marker; sc evenly across ends of rows; working in sts on last row, 2 sc in first hdc, sc in each st across to last hdc, 2 sc in last hdc; join with slip st to first sc, finish off.

Design by Sarah J. Green.

Doily Rug

EASY

Finished Size: 35½" (90 cm) diameter

SHOPPING LIST

Yarn (Bulky Weight) 5 BULKY
[3.5 ounces, 95 yards
(100 grams, 86 meters) per skein]:
☐ 6 skeins

Crochet Hook
☐ Size M/N (9 mm)
or size needed for gauge

GAUGE INFORMATION

Gauge Swatch: 7" (17.75 cm) diameter
Work same as Body through Rnd 4:
14 ch-3 sps

BODY

Ch 7; join with slip st to form a ring.

Rnd 1 (Right side)**:** Ch 5 **(counts as first dc plus ch 2, now and throughout)**, (dc in ring, ch 2) 13 times; join with slip st to first dc: 14 dc and 14 ch-2 sps.

Note: Loop a short piece of yarn around any stitch to mark Rnd 1 as **right** side.

Rnd 2: Ch 3 **(counts as first dc, now and throughout)**, 2 dc in next ch-2 sp, (dc in next dc, 2 dc in next ch-2 sp) around; join with slip st to first dc: 42 dc.

Rnd 3: Ch 1, sc in sp **before** joining ***(Fig. A)***, ★ ch 3, skip next 3 dc, sc in sp **before** next dc; repeat from ★ around to last 3 dc, ch 1, skip last 3 dc, hdc in first sc to form last ch-3 sp: 14 ch-3 sps.

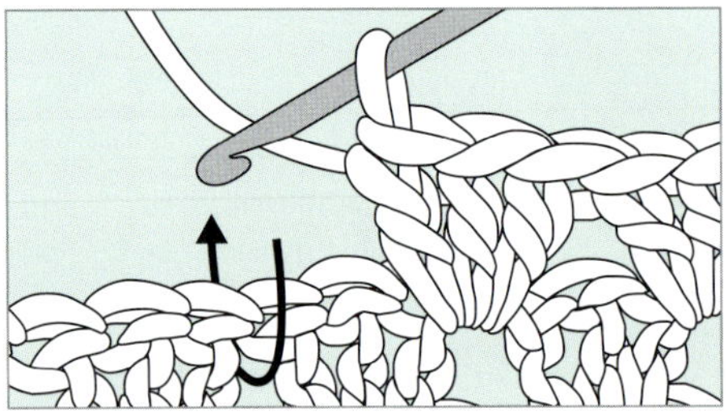

Fig. A

Rnd 4: Ch 1, 2 sc in last ch-3 sp made, (ch 3, 2 sc in next ch-3 sp) around, ch 1, hdc in first sc to form last ch-3 sp.

Rnd 5: Ch 5, dc in last ch-3 sp made, ch 2, (dc, ch 2) twice in next ch-3 sp and in each ch-3 sp around; join with slip st to first dc: 28 ch-2 sps.

Rnd 6: Slip st in next ch-2 sp, ch 6 **(counts as first dc plus ch 3, now and throughout)**, (dc in next ch-2 sp, ch 3) around; join with slip st to first dc.

Rnd 7: (Slip st, ch 3, 3 dc) in next ch-3 sp, 4 dc in next ch-3 sp and in each ch-3 sp around; join with slip st to first dc: 112 dc.

Rnd 8: Ch 1, sc in sp **before** joining, ch 7, skip next 4 dc, ★ sc in sp **before** next dc, ch 7, skip next 4 dc; repeat from ★ around; join with slip st to first sc: 28 ch-7 sps.

Rnd 9: (Slip st, ch 3, 8 dc) in next ch-7 sp, sc in next ch-7 sp, ★ 9 dc in next ch-7 sp, sc in next ch-7 sp; repeat from ★ around; join with slip st to first dc: 140 sts.

Rnd 10: Ch 1, sc in same st as joining, (ch 4, skip next 3 dc, sc in next dc) twice, ★ ch 4, skip next sc, sc in next dc, (ch 4, skip next 3 dc, sc in next dc) twice; repeat from ★ around to last sc, ch 1, skip last sc, dc in first sc to form last ch-4 sp: 42 ch-4 sps.

Rnd 11: Ch 5, dc in last ch-4 sp made, ch 2, (dc, ch 2) twice in next ch-4 sp and in each ch-4 sp around; join with slip st to first dc: 84 ch-2 sps.

Rnd 12: Slip st in next ch-2 sp, ch 6, skip next ch-2 sp, dc in next ch-2 sp, ★ ch 3, skip next ch-2 sp, dc in next ch-2 sp; repeat from ★ around to last ch-2 sp, ch 1, skip last ch-2 sp, hdc in first dc to form last ch-3 sp: 42 ch-3 sps.

Rnd 13: Ch 3, dc in last ch-3 sp made, ch 1, ★ (2 dc, ch 2, 2 dc) in next ch-3 sp, ch 1; repeat from ★ around, 2 dc in same sp as first dc, ch 1, sc in first dc to form last ch-2 sp: 84 sps.

Rnd 14: Ch 3, dc in last ch-2 sp made, sc in next ch-1 sp, ★ (2 dc, ch 2, 2 dc) in next ch-2 sp, sc in next ch-1 sp; repeat from ★ around, 2 dc in same sp as first dc, ch 1, sc in first dc to form last ch-2 sp: 42 ch-2 sps.

Rnd 15: Ch 3, dc in last ch-2 sp made, ch 1, (2 dc, ch 1) twice in next ch-2 sp and in each ch-2 sp around, 2 dc in same sp as first dc, sc in first dc to form last ch-1 sp: 84 ch-1 sps.

Rnd 16: Ch 3, dc in last ch-1 sp made, sc in next ch-1 sp, ★ (2 dc, ch 2, 2 dc) in next ch-1 sp, sc in next ch-1 sp; repeat from ★ around, 2 dc in same sp as first dc, ch 1, sc in first dc to form last ch-2 sp: 42 ch-2 sps.

Rnd 17: Ch 3, dc in last ch-2 sp made, ch 1, ★ (2 dc, ch 2, 2 dc) in next ch-2 sp, ch 1; repeat from ★ around, 2 dc in same sp as first dc, ch 1, sc in first dc to form last ch-2 sp: 84 sps.

Rnd 18: Ch 3, dc in last ch-2 sp made, sc in next ch-1 sp, ★ (2 dc, ch 2, 2 dc) in next ch-2 sp, sc in next ch-1 sp; repeat from ★ around, 2 dc in same sp as first dc, ch 1, sc in first dc to form last ch-2 sp: 42 ch-2 sps.

Rnd 19: Ch 3, dc in last ch-2 sp made, ch 2, (2 dc, ch 2) twice in next ch-2 sp and in each ch-2 sp around, 2 dc in same sp as first dc, ch 1, sc in first dc to form last ch-2 sp: 84 ch-2 sps.

Rnd 20: Ch 3, dc in last ch-2 sp made, ch 1, sc in next ch-2 sp, ch 1, ★ (2 dc, ch 2, 2 dc) in next ch-2 sp, ch 1, sc in next ch-2 sp, ch 1; repeat from ★ around, 2 dc in same sp as first dc, ch 1, sc in first dc to form last ch-2 sp: 210 sts and 126 sps.

Rnd 21: Ch 1, sc in last ch-2 sp made and in next 2 dc and next ch-1 sp, skip next sc, sc in next ch-1 sp and in next 2 dc, ★ (sc, ch 3, sc) in next ch-2 sp, sc in next 2 dc and in next ch-1 sp, skip next sc, sc in next ch-1 sp and in next 2 dc; repeat from ★ around, sc in same sp as first sc, ch 3; join with slip st to first sc, finish off.

Design by Sue Galucki.

Lazy Puff Stitch Rug

EASY

Finished Size: 39½" wide x 23" deep (100.5 cm x 58.5 cm)

SHOPPING LIST

Yarn (Super Bulky Weight) SUPER BULKY 6
[4 ounces, 64 yards (113 grams, 59 meters) per skein]:
☐ 8 skeins

Crochet Hook
☐ Size Q (16 mm) **or** size needed for gauge

Additional Supplies
☐ Puffy fabric paint (optional)

GAUGE INFORMATION

Gauge Swatch: 8" wide x 4" high (20.5 cm x 10 cm)

Work same as Rug for 2 rows: 5 Puff Sts, 3 dc, and one ch-1 sp.

STITCH GUIDE

PUFF ST (uses one st or sp)
Dc in st or sp indicated, ★ YO, insert hook around post of dc just made ***(Fig. A)***, YO and pull up a loop, YO and draw through 2 loops on hook; repeat from ★ 2 times **more**, YO and draw through all 4 loops on hook.

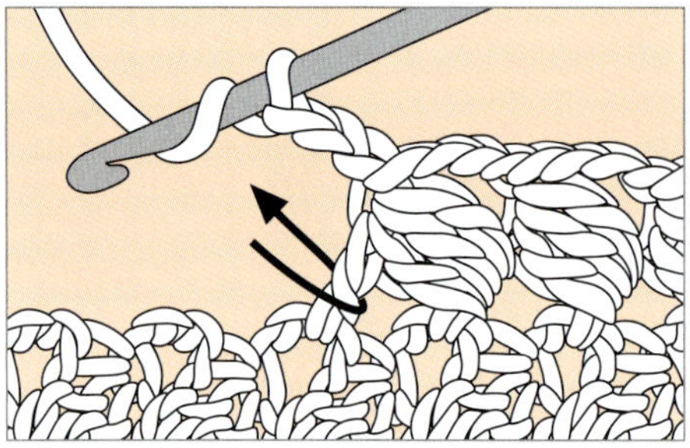

Fig. A

BODY

Row 1 (Wrong side)**:** Holding two strands of yarn together, ch 4, 6 dc in fourth ch from hook **(3 skipped chs count as one dc)**: 7 dc.

Row 2: Ch 4 **(counts as first dc plus ch 1, now and throughout)**, turn; work Puff Sts in each of next 5 dc, 2 dc in last dc: 5 Puff Sts, 3 dc, and one ch-1 sp.

Row 3: Ch 4, turn; work Puff St in next dc, work Puff St in ch-3 sp of next Puff St across to next ch-1 sp, dc in next ch-1 sp and in last dc: 6 Puff Sts, 3 dc, and one ch-1 sp.

Row 4: Ch 4, turn; work Puff St in next dc, ★ work 2 Puff Sts in ch-3 sp of next Puff St, work Puff St in ch-3 sp of next Puff St; 2 times **more**, dc in next ch-1 sp and in last dc: 10 Puff Sts, 3 dc, and one ch-1 sp.

Row 5: Ch 4, turn; work Puff St in next dc and in ch-3 sp of next Puff St, ★ work 2 Puff Sts in ch-3 sp of next Puff St, work Puff St in ch-3 sps of next 2 Puff Sts; repeat from ★ 2 times **more**, dc in next ch-1 sp and in last dc: 14 Puff Sts, 3 dc, and one ch-1 sp.

Row 6: Ch 4, turn; work Puff St in next dc and in ch-3 sp of each Puff St across to next ch-1 sp, dc in next ch-1 sp and in last dc: 15 Puff Sts, 3 dc, and one ch-1 sp.

Row 7: Ch 4, turn; work Puff St in next dc and in ch-3 sps of next 2 Puff Sts, work 2 Puff Sts in ch-3 sp of next Puff St, ★ work Puff St in ch-3 sps of next 3 Puff Sts, work 2 Puff Sts in ch-3 sp of next Puff St; repeat from ★ once **more**, work Puff St in ch-3 sps of next 4 Puff Sts, dc in next ch-1 sp and in last dc: 19 Puff Sts, 3 dc, and one ch-1 sp.

Row 8: Ch 4, turn; work Puff St in next dc and in ch-3 sps of next 3 Puff Sts, work 2 Puff Sts in ch-3 sp of next Puff St, ★ work Puff St in ch-3 sps of next 4 Puff Sts, work 2 Puff Sts in ch-3 sp of next Puff St; repeat from ★ once **more**, work Puff St in ch-3 sps of next 5 Puff Sts, dc in next ch-1 sp and in last dc: 23 Puff Sts, 3 dc, and one ch-1 sp.

Row 9: Ch 4, turn; work Puff St in next dc and in ch-3 sps of next 4 Puff Sts, work 2 Puff Sts in ch-3 sp of next Puff St, ★ work Puff St in ch-3 sps of next 5 Puff Sts, work 2 Puff Sts in ch-3 sp of next Puff St; repeat from ★ once **more**, work Puff St in ch-3 sps of next 6 Puff Sts, dc in next ch-1 sp and in last dc: 27 Puff Sts, 3 dc, and one ch-1 sp.

Edging Rnd: Ch 4, turn; work Puff St in next dc and in ch-3 sps of next 5 Puff Sts, work 2 Puff Sts in ch-3 sp of next Puff St, ★ work Puff St in ch-3 sps of next 6 Puff Sts, work 2 Puff Sts in ch-3 sp of next Puff St; repeat from ★ once **more**, work Puff St in ch-3 sps of next 7 Puff Sts, dc in next ch-1 sp and in last dc; work Puff St in end of each row across; join with slip st to dc of first Puff St, finish off.

Optional: Paint large dots on wrong side of rug for a non-slip surface.

Design by Karen Barnes.

Skyline

EASY

Finished Size: 60" x 74" (152.5 cm x 188 cm)

SHOPPING LIST

Yarn (Medium Weight) 4
[3.5 ounces, 208 yards (100 grams, 190 meters) per skein]:
- ☐ Gray - 9 skeins
- ☐ Navy - 8 skeins

Crochet Hook
- ☐ Size I (5.5 mm) **or** size needed for gauge

GAUGE INFORMATION

In pattern,
12 sts and Rows 1-10 = 4" (10 cm);
Gauge Swatch: 4" (10 cm) square
With Gray, ch 16.
Rows 1-10: Work same as Body: 14 sc.
Finish off.

STITCH GUIDE

TREBLE CROCHET ***(abbreviated tr)***
YO twice, insert hook in st indicated, YO and pull up a loop (4 loops on hook), (YO and draw through 2 loops on hook) 3 times.

DOUBLE TREBLE CROCHET ***(abbreviated dtr)***
YO 3 times, insert hook in st indicated, YO and pull up a loop (5 loops on hook), (YO and draw through 2 loops on hook) 4 times.

FRONT POST DOUBLE CROCHET ***(abbreviated FPdc)***
YO, working in **front** of next sc, insert hook from **front** to **back** around post of st indicated *(Fig. 6, page 124)*, YO and pull up a loop (3 loops on hook), (YO and draw through 2 loops on hook) twice. Skip sc behind FPdc.

BODY

With Gray, ch 168, place marker in third ch from hook for st placement.

Row 1 (Right side)**:** Dc in fourth ch from hook **(3 skipped chs count as first dc)** and in each ch across, changing to Navy in last dc *(Fig. 7d, page 124)*: 166 dc.

Note: Loop a short piece of yarn around any stitch to mark Row 1 as **right** side.

Row 2: Ch 1, turn; sc in each dc across.

Row 3: Ch 3 **(counts as first dc, now and throughout)**, turn; ★ dc in next 4 sc, ch 4, skip next 4 sc; repeat from ★ across to last 5 sc, dc in last 5 sc: 86 dc and 80 chs.

Row 4: Ch 1, turn; sc in each dc and in each ch across changing to Gray in last sc: 166 sc.

Row 5: Ch 3, turn; dc in next sc, work FPdc around each of next 2 dc one row **below**, ★ dc in next sc, working in **front** of previous 2 rows, dtr in 4 skipped sc on Row 2, dc in next sc on Row 4, work FPdc around each of next 2 dc one row **below**; repeat from ★ across to last 2 sc, dc in last 2 sc changing to Navy in last dc.

Row 6: Ch 1, turn; sc in each st across.

Row 7: Ch 7 **(counts as first dc plus ch 4)**, turn; skip next 4 sc, ★ dc in next 4 sc, ch 4, skip next 4 sc; repeat from ★ across to last sc, dc in last sc: 82 dc and 84 chs.

Row 8: Ch 1, turn; sc in each dc and in each ch across changing to Gray in last sc: 166 sc.

Row 9: Ch 3, turn; working in **front** of previous 2 rows, dtr in 4 skipped sc on Row 6, ★ dc in next sc, work FPdc around each of next 2 dc one row **below**, dc in next sc, working in **front** of previous 2 rows, dtr in 4 skipped sc on Row 6; repeat from ★ across to last sc, dc in last sc changing to Navy.

Rows 10-173: Repeat Rows 2-9, 20 times; then repeat Rows 2-5 once **more**; at end of Row 173, do **not** change colors.

BORDER

Rnd 1: Ch 1, do **not** turn; 2 sc in last dc made; work 212 sc evenly spaced across ends of rows; working in free loops of beginning ch *(Fig. 5b, page 124)*, 3 sc in first ch, sc in each ch across to marked ch, 3 sc in marked ch, remove marker; work 212 sc evenly spaced across ends of rows, 3 sc in first dc on Row 173, sc in each st across and in same st as first sc; join with slip st to first sc: 764 sc.

Rnd 2: Ch 4 (**counts as first tr**), 2 tr in same st as joining, ★ tr in next sc and in each sc across to center sc of next corner 3-sc group, 5 tr in center sc; repeat from ★ 2 times **more**, tr in next sc and in each sc across, 2 tr in same st as first tr; join with slip t to first tr changing to Navy *(Fig. 7a, page 124)*: 780 tr.

Rnd 3: Ch 3, 2 dc in same st as joining, ★ dc in next tr and in each tr across to center tr of next corner 5-tr group, 5 dc in center tr; repeat from ★ 2 times **more**, dc in next tr and in each tr around, 2 dc in same st as first dc; join with slip st to first dc changing to Gray: 796 dc.

Rnd 4: Ch 2 (**counts as first hdc**), 2 hdc in same st as joining, ★ hdc in next dc and in each dc across to center dc of next corner 5-dc group, 5 hdc in center dc; repeat from ★ 2 times **more**, hdc in next dc and in each dc across, 2 hdc in same st as first hdc; join with slip st to first hdc changing to Navy: 812 hdc.

Rnd 5: Ch 1, sc in same st as joining, ch 1, (sc in next hdc, ch 1) around; join with slip st to first sc, finish off.

Design by Janet Akins.

Slanted Stripes

EASY

Finished Size: 46" x 64¾"
(117 cm x 164.5 cm)

SHOPPING LIST

Yarn (Medium Weight Cotton) MEDIUM 4
[2.5 ounces, 120 yards
(71 grams, 109 meters) per skein]:
- ☐ White - 13 skeins
- ☐ Blue - 4 skeins
- ☐ Tan - 4 skeins

Crochet Hook
- ☐ Size I (5.5 mm)
or size needed for gauge

GAUGE INFORMATION

In pattern,
9 rows = 6" (15.25 cm);
9 Blocks = 8" (20.25 cm)
Gauge Swatch: 8" wide x 6" high
(20.25 cm x 15.25 cm)
Work same as Body through Row 9:
9 Blocks.

STITCH GUIDE

BEGINNING BLOCK
Ch 4, turn; hdc in third ch from hook and in last ch.

BLOCK
Slip st in ch-2 sp of previous Block, ch 2, 2 hdc in same sp.

Throw is worked diagonally from corner to corner.

BODY

Row 1 (Right side)**:** With Tan, ch 4, hdc in third ch from hook and in last ch: one Block.

Note: Loop a short piece of yarn around any stitch to mark Row 1 as **right** side.

Row 2: Work Beginning Block, slip st in ch-2 sp on first Block, ch 2, 2 hdc in same sp: 2 Blocks.

Row 3: Work Beginning Block, slip st in ch-2 sp on first Block, ch 2, 2 hdc in same sp, work Block: 3 Blocks.

Rows 4-13: Work Beginning Block, slip st in ch-2 sp on first Block, ch 2, 2 hdc in same sp, work Blocks across: 13 Blocks.

Row 14: Work Beginning Block, slip st in ch-2 sp on first Block, ch 2, 2 hdc in same sp, work Blocks across changing to White in last hdc made ***(Fig. 7c, page 124)***; cut Tan: 14 Blocks.

Rows 15-66: Continue established pattern working in the following stripe sequence: 2 Rows White, 10 rows Tan, 4 rows White, 8 rows Tan, 6 rows White, 6 rows Tan, 8 rows White, 4 rows Tan, 4 rows White; at end of Row 66, do **not** change colors: 66 Blocks.

To form length of Throw, one side edge will decrease one Block and the opposite side edge will increase one Block per row, maintaining 66 Blocks.

Row 67: Work Beginning Block, slip st in ch-2 sp on first Block, ch 2, 2 hdc in same sp, work Blocks across to last Block, slip st in ch-2 sp on last Block.

Row 68: Turn; slip st in first 2 hdc and in next ch-2 sp, ch 2, 2 hdc in same sp, work Blocks across.

Rows 69-72: Repeat Rows 67 and 68 twice; at end of Row 72, change to Tan in last hdc made; cut White.

Rows 73-94: Continue to repeat Rows 67 and 68 for pattern in the following stripe sequence: 2 Rows Tan, 12 rows White, 2 rows Blue, 6 rows White; at end of Row 94, do **not** change colors.

To form width of Throw, one Block is decreased at the beginning and at the end of each row.

Row 95 (Decrease row)**:** Turn; slip st in first 2 hdc and in next ch-2 sp, ch 2, 2 hdc in same sp, work Blocks across to last Block, slip st in ch-2 sp on last Block: 65 Blocks.

Rows 96 and 97: Repeat Row 95 twice; at end of Row 97, change to Blue in last slip st ***(Fig. A)***; cut White: 63 Blocks.

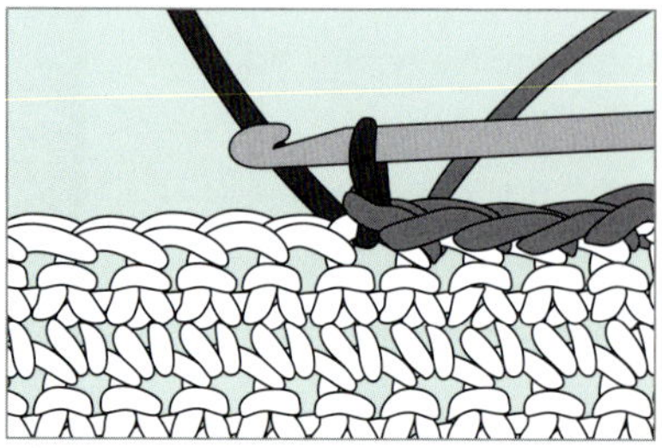

Fig. A

Rows 98-157: Repeat Row 95 for pattern in the following stripe sequence: 4 Rows Blue, 8 rows White, 6 rows Blue, 6 rows White, 8 rows Blue, 4 rows White, 10 rows Blue, 2 rows White, 12 rows Blue; at end of Row 157, do **not** change colors: 3 Blocks.

Row 158: Turn; slip st in first 2 hdc and in next ch-2 sp, ch 2, 2 hdc in same sp, work Block, slip st in ch-2 sp on last Block: 2 Blocks.

Row 159: Turn; slip st in first 2 hdc and in next ch-2 sp, ch 2, 2 hdc in same sp, slip st in ch-2 sp on last Block; finish off: one Block.

EDGING

Rnd 1: With **right** side facing, join White with slip st in any corner; ch 1, 3 hdc in same sp, hdc evenly around entire Body, working 3 hdc in each corner; join with slip st to Back Loop Only of first hdc ***(Fig. 4, page 124)***.

Rnds 2 and 3: Ch 1, working in Back Loops Only, sc in each st around, working 3 sc in center st of each corner 3-st group; join with slip st to first sc.

Finish off.

Design by Cheryl Riley.

Striped Set

EASY

Finished Sizes:
Afghan - 48" x 64" (122 cm x 162.5 cm)
Pillow - 16" (40.5 cm) square

SHOPPING LIST

Yarn (Bulky Weight) 5
[5 ounces, 153 yards
(140 grams, 140 meters) per skein]:

Afghan
- ☐ Off White - 8 skeins
- ☐ Dk Purple - 6 skeins

Pillow
- ☐ Off White - 2 skeins
- ☐ Dk Purple - 1 skein

Crochet Hook
- ☐ Size K (6.5 mm)
  or size needed for gauge

Additional Supplies
- ☐ 16" (40.5 cm) square pillow form
- ☐ Yarn needle

GAUGE INFORMATION

13 dc = 5" (12.75 cm);
11 rows = 8" (20.25 cm)
One Square = 16" (40.5 cm)
Gauge Swatch: 5"w x 4¼"h
(12.75 cm x 10.75 cm)
With Off White, ch 15.
Row 1: Dc in fourth ch from hook **(3 skipped chs count as first dc)** and in each ch across: 13 dc.
Rows 2-6: Ch 3 **(counts as first dc)**, turn; dc in next dc and in each dc across.
Finish off.

Afghan

Square (Make 12)

With Off White, ch 44.

Row 1 (Right side)**:** Dc in fourth ch from hook **(3 skipped chs count as first dc)** and in each ch across: 42 dc.

Note: Loop a short piece of yarn around any stitch to mark Row 1 as **right** side.

Row 2: Ch 3 **(counts as first dc, now and throughout)**, turn; dc in next dc and in each dc across changing to Dk Purple in last dc ***(Fig. 7d, page 124)***.

Row 3: Ch 3, turn; dc in next dc and in each dc across.

Row 4: Ch 3, turn; dc in next dc and in each dc across changing to Off White in last dc.

Row 5: Ch 3, turn; dc in next dc and in each dc across.

Row 6: Ch 3, turn; dc in next dc and in each dc across changing to Dk Purple in last dc.

Rows 7-22: Repeat Rows 3-6, 4 times; at end of Row 22, do **not** change to Dk Purple.

Finish off.

ASSEMBLY

With Off White and using diagram as a guide, sew Squares together, forming 3 horizontal strips of 4 Squares each; then sew strips together.

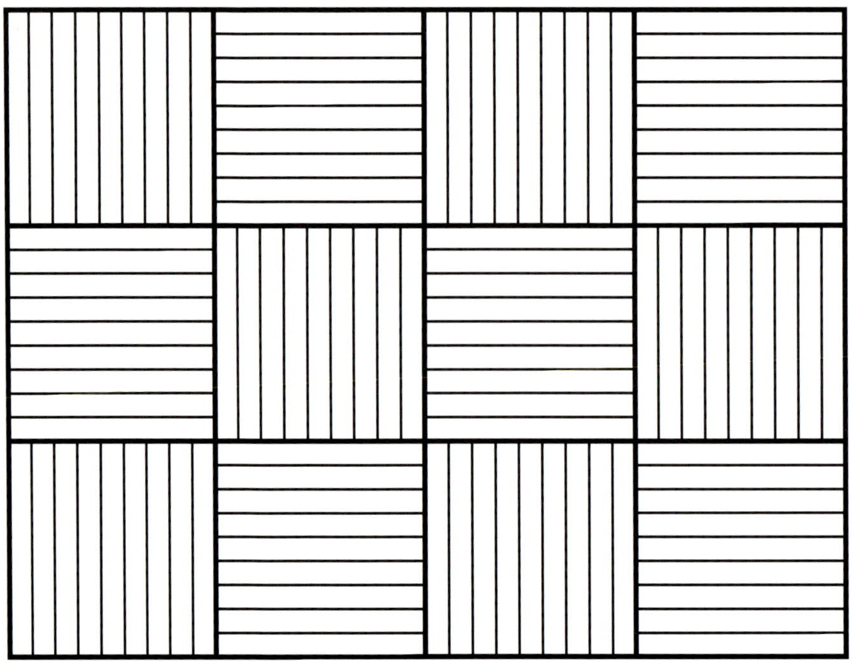

Pillow

Square (Make 2)

Work same as Afghan Square.

ASSEMBLY

With **wrong** sides together and alternating direction of stripes on each side, sew 3 sides of Squares together; insert pillow form and sew remaining side closed.

Designs by Melissa Leapman.

Diagonal Set

EASY

Finished Sizes:
Afghan - 48" x 64" (122 cm x 162.5 cm)
Pillow - 16" (40.5 cm) square

SHOPPING LIST

Yarn (Bulky Weight) BULKY 5
[5 ounces, 155 yards
(140 grams, 142 meters) per skein]:

Afghan
- ☐ Black - 10 skeins
- ☐ White - 10 skeins

Pillow
- ☐ Black - 2 skeins
- ☐ White - 2 skeins

Crochet Hook
- ☐ Size K (6.5 mm)
  or size needed for gauge

Additional Supplies
- ☐ 16" (40.5 cm) square pillow form
- ☐ Yarn needle

GAUGE INFORMATION

In pattern,
11 sts and 12 rows = 4" (10 cm)
One Square = 16" (40.5 cm)

Gauge Swatch: 4" (10 cm) square
With White, ch 12.
Row 1: Sc in second ch from hook and in each ch across: 11 sc.
Rows 2-12: Ch 1, turn; sc in each sc across.
Finish off.

STITCH GUIDE

BEGINNING DECREASE (uses first 2 sts)
YO, insert hook in first st, YO and pull up a loop (3 loops on hook), pull up a loop in next sc, YO and draw through all 4 loops on hook.

DECREASE (uses next 2 sts)
Pull up a loop in next sc (2 loops on hook), YO, insert hook in next st, YO and pull up a loop, YO and draw through all 4 loops on hook.

Afghan

Square (Make 12)

Row 1: With White, ch 2, 2 sc in second ch from hook: 2 sc.

Row 2 (Right side)**:** Ch 1, turn; (hdc, sc) in first sc, (sc, hdc) in last sc: 4 sts.

Note: Loop a short piece of yarn around any stitch to mark Row 2 as **right** side.

Row 3: Ch 1, turn; (hdc, sc) in first hdc, sc in next 2 sc, (sc, hdc) in last hdc: 6 sts.

Rows 4-32: Ch 1, turn; (hdc, sc) in first hdc, sc in each sc across to last hdc, (sc, hdc) in last hdc: 64 sts.

Row 33: Ch 1, turn; (hdc, sc) in first hdc, sc in each sc across to last hdc, (sc, hdc) in last hdc changing to Black in last hdc made ***(Fig. 7c, page 124)***: 66 sts.

Rows 34-64: Ch 1, turn; work beginning decrease, sc in next sc and in each sc across to last 2 sts, decrease: 4 sts.

Row 65: Ch 1, turn; work beginning decrease, decrease: 2 sts.

Row 66: Ch 1, turn; pull up a loop in each of first 2 sts, YO and draw through all 3 loops on hook; finish off leaving a long end for sewing: one st.

ASSEMBLY

With **wrong** sides together and using diagram as a guide, sew Squares together forming 3 vertical strips of 4 Squares each; then sew strips together in same manner.

Pillow

Square (Make 2)

Work same as Afghan Square.

ASSEMBLY

With **wrong** sides together, sew 3 sides of Squares together; insert pillow form and sew remaining side closed.

Designs by Melissa Leapman.

PRIVATE DREAMS
OF PUBLIC PEOPLE

Triangle Pillow Set

EASY

Finished Sizes:
Pillow - 18" (45.5 cm) square
Floor Pillow - 28½" wide x 45½" long x 5½" deep (72.5 cm x 115.5 cm x 14 cm)

SHOPPING LIST

Yarn (Super Bulky Weight) SUPER BULKY 6
[6 ounces, 106 yards (170 grams, 97 meters) per skein]:

Pillow
- ☐ Brown - 2 skeins
- ☐ Green - 2 skeins
- ☐ Ecru - 2 skeins

Floor Pillow
- ☐ Brown - 10 skeins
- ☐ Green - 7 skeins
- ☐ Ecru - 7 skeins

Crochet Hook
- ☐ Size N/P (10 mm) **or** size needed for gauge

Additional Supplies
- ☐ Yarn needle
- ☐ 18" (45.5 cm) square pillow form (Pillow only)
- ☐ Safety pins (Floor Pillow only)
- ☐ 20" x 54" (51 cm x 137 cm) body pillows - 2 (Floor Pillow only)
- ☐ Sewing needle and thread (Floor Pillow only)

GAUGE INFORMATION

Each Triangle = 4¾" wide x 4¾" tall (12 cm x 12 cm)
Gauge Swatch: 4¾" wide x 4¾" tall (12 cm x 12 cm)
Work same as Triangle: 27 sc.

Pillow

TRIANGLE Make 48 **total**
(16 **each** Brown, Green, and Ecru)

Ch 10.

Row 1 (Right side)**:** Sc in second ch from hook and in each ch across: 9 sc.

Note: Loop a short piece of yarn around any stitch to mark Row 1 as **right** side.

Rows 2-7: Ch 1 (**counts as first sc, now and through Row 8**), turn; sc in next sc and in each sc across to last sc, leave last sc unworked: 3 sc.

Row 8: Ch 1, turn; sc in next sc, leave last sc unworked: 2 sc.

Edging: Ch 1, turn; sc in first 2 sc; skip first row, sc in end of next 7 rows; working in free loops of beginning ch ***(Fig. 5b, page 124)***; 2 sc in first ch, sc in next 7 chs, 2 sc in next ch; sc in end of first 7 rows, skip last row; join with slip st to first sc, finish off: 27 sc.

FINISHING

Place Triangles as desired or use diagram as a guide for placement to match Floor Pillow. With **wrong** sides together and working through inside loops **only**, whipstitch Triangles together ***(Fig. 12b, page 126)***, forming 4 horizontal strips of 12 Triangles each. Whipstitch strips together in same manner, then whipstitch ends of strips together to form a tube.

Flatten tube, then whipstitch top and bottom seams, inserting pillow form before closing.

Every day may
not be good,
but there's something
good with every day
that I can crochet.

Floor Pillow

TRIANGLE Make 216 **total**

(72 **each** Brown, Green, and Ecru)

Work same as Pillow Triangle, page 53: 27 sc.

SIDE (Make 2)

With Brown, ch 12.

Row 1 (Right side)**:** Sc in second ch from hook and in each ch across: 11 sc.

Note: Mark Row 1 as **right** side.

Row 2: Ch 1, turn; sc in each sc across.

Repeat Row 2 for pattern until piece measures approximately 45½" (115.5 cm) from beginning ch, ending by working a **wrong** side row.

Edging: Ch 1, turn; 2 sc in first sc, sc in next 9 sc, 3 sc in last sc; sc evenly across ends of rows; working in free loops of beginning ch, 3 sc in first ch, sc in next 9 chs, 3 sc in next ch; sc evenly across ends of rows; join with slip st to first sc, finish off leaving a long for sewing.

FINISHING

Using diagram as a guide for placement, with **wrong** sides together, and working through inside loops **only**, whipstitch Triangles together ***(Fig. 12b, page 126)***, forming 6 horizontal strips of 36 Triangles each.

Whipstitch strips together in same manner, then whipstitch ends of strips together to form a large tube.

Flatten tube. Pin one Side to one long edge of tube, centering short ends of Side to center Triangles at flattened edges and corners of Side to tips of Triangles on each side of center Triangles. Using long end, whipstitch Side to tube.

To prevent the body pillows from shifting inside the Floor Pillow, sew the long edges of the pillows together.

Whipstitch remaining Side to opposite long edge in same manner, inserting pillows before closing.

Designs by Ashley Leither.

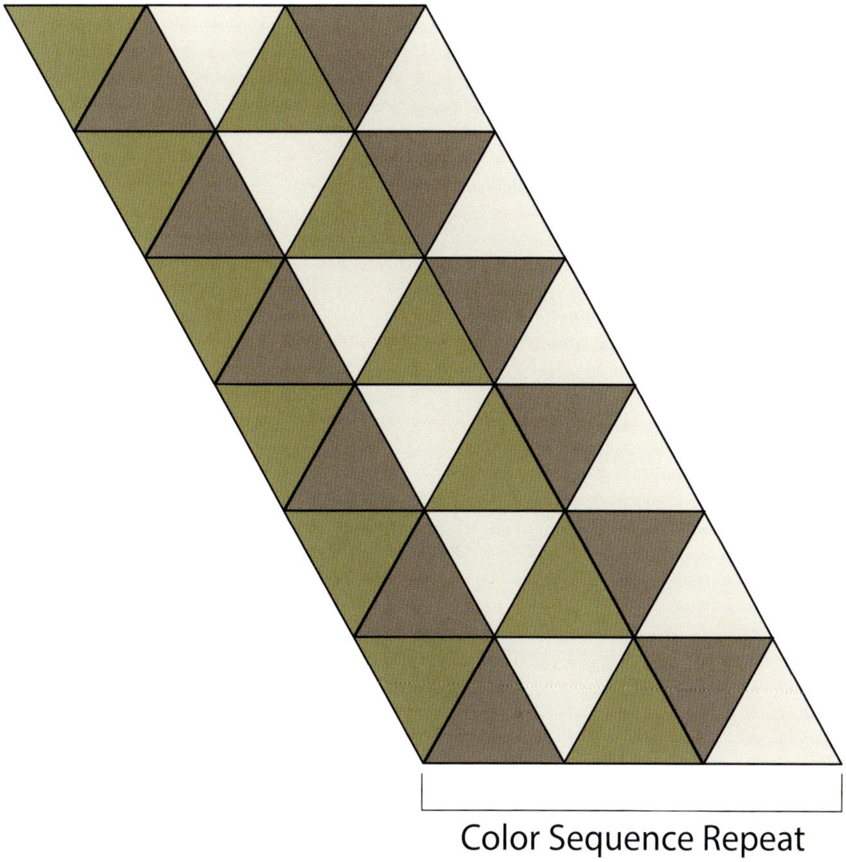

Batchelor Buttons

EASY

Finished Size: 20" (51 cm) square

SHOPPING LIST

Yarn (Medium Weight) MEDIUM 4
[4 ounces, 186 yards
(113 grams, 170 meters) per skein]:

- ☐ Blue - 2 skeins
- ☐ Rust - 1 skein
- ☐ Yellow - 1 skein
- ☐ Orange - 1 skein
- ☐ Brown - 1 skein

Crochet Hook

- ☐ Size H (5 mm)
  or size needed for gauge

Additional Supplies

- ☐ 20" (51 cm) square pillow form
- ☐ $^5/_8$" (16 mm) buttons - 5
- ☐ Sewing needle and thread
- ☐ Yarn needle

GAUGE INFORMATION

In pattern, 16 sc and 16 rows = 4" (10 cm)
Gauge Swatch: 4" (10 cm) square
With Blue, ch 17.
Work same as Back on page 58 for 16 rows.
Finish off.

STITCH GUIDE

TREBLE CROCHET ***(abbreviated tr)***
YO twice, insert hook in sp indicated, YO and pull up a loop (4 loops on hook), (YO and draw through 2 loops on hook) 3 times.

DOUBLE TREBLE CROCHET ***(abbreviated dtr)***
YO 3 times, insert hook in sp indicated, YO and pull up a loop (5 loops on hook), (YO and draw through 2 loops on hook) 4 times.

FRONT

With Blue, ch 81.

Row 1 (Right side)**:** Sc in second ch from hook and in each ch across: 80 sc.

Note: Loop a short piece of yarn around any stitch to mark Row 1 as **right** side.

Row 2: Ch 1, turn; sc in first sc, sc in Front Loop Only of next sc and each sc across to last sc ***(Fig. 4, page 124)***, sc in **both** loops of last sc.

Row 3: Ch 1, turn; sc in first sc, sc in Back Loop Only of next sc and each sc across to last sc, sc in **both** loops of last sc.

Rows 4-10: Repeat Rows 2 and 3, 3 times; then repeat Row 2 once **more**.

Row 11: Ch 1, turn; sc in first sc, ch 1, ★ skip next sc, sc in Back Loop Only of next sc, ch 1; repeat from ★ 21 times **more**, skip next sc, sc in Back Loop Only of each sc across to last sc, sc in **both** loops of last sc: 57 sc and 23 chs.

Row 12: Ch 1, turn; sc in first sc, sc in Front Loop Only of each sc and each ch across to last sc, sc in **both** loops of last sc: 80 sc.

Row 13: Ch 1, turn; sc in first sc, sc in Back Loop Only of next sc and each sc across to last sc, sc in **both** loops of last sc.

Rows 14-24: Repeat Rows 2 and 3, 5 times; then repeat Row 2 once **more**.

Row 25: Ch 1, turn; sc in first sc, ch 1, ★ skip next sc, sc in Back Loop Only of next sc, ch 1; repeat from ★ 24 times **more**, skip next sc, sc in Back Loop Only of each sc across to last sc, sc in **both** loops of last sc: 54 sc and 26 chs.

Rows 26-38: Repeat Rows 12-24.

Row 39: Ch 1, turn; sc in first sc, ch 1, ★ skip next sc, sc in Back Loop Only of next sc, ch 1; repeat from ★ 19 times **more**, skip next sc, sc in Back Loop Only of each sc across to last sc, sc in **both** loops of last sc: 59 sc and 21 chs.

Rows 40-52: Repeat Rows 12-24.

Row 53: Ch 1, turn; sc in first sc, ch 1, ★ skip next sc, sc in Back Loop Only of next sc, ch 1; repeat from ★ 16 times **more**, skip next sc, sc in Back Loop Only of each sc across to last sc, sc in **both** loops of last sc: 62 sc and 18 chs.

Rows 54-66: Repeat Rows 12-24.

Row 67: Ch 1, turn; sc in first sc, ch 1, ★ skip next sc, sc in Back Loop Only of next sc, ch 1; repeat from ★ 8 times **more**, skip next sc, sc in Back Loop Only of each sc across to last sc, sc in **both** loops of last sc: 70 sc and 10 chs.

Rows 68-80: Repeat Rows 12-24.

Row 81: Ch 1, turn; sc in first sc, sc in Back Loop Only of next sc and each sc across to last sc, sc in both loops of last sc; finish off.

FLOWER

(Make 5 - 2 **each** Yellow and Rust, and one Orange)

Ch 4; join with slip st to form a ring.

Rnd 1 (Right side)**:** Ch 3 **(counts as first dc)**, (8 dc, tr, 2 dtr, tr, sc) in ring; join with slip st to first dc, finish off leaving long end for sewing.

Note: Mark Rnd 1 as **right** side.

STEM

With **right** side of Front facing and beginning ch to your left, insert hook in first st on Row 11 from **front** to **back**, holding Brown on **wrong** side, YO and pull up a loop, ★ insert hook in next ch-1 sp, YO and draw though sp and loop on hook; repeat from ★ across; finish off.

Repeat for Rows 25, 39, 53, and 67.

Thread needle with long end and using photo as a guide, sew one Flower to top of each Stem.

Sew button to center of each Flower.

BACK

With Blue, ch 81.

Row 1 (Right side)**:** Sc in second ch from hook and in each ch across. 80 sc.

Note: Mark Row 1 as **right** side.

Row 2: Ch 1, turn; sc in first sc, sc in Front Loop Only of next sc and each sc across to last sc, sc in **both** loops of last sc.

Row 3: Ch 1, turn; sc in first sc, sc in Back Loop Only of next sc and each sc across to last sc, sc in **both** loops of last sc.

Rows 4-81: Repeat Rows 2 and 3, 39 times.

Finish off.

JOINING

With **wrong** sides and last rows of Front and Back together, Front facing, and working through **both** layers, join Blue with sc in first sc on last row ***(see Joining With Sc, page 123)***; sc evenly around working (sc, ch 1, sc) in each corner and inserting pillow form before closing; join with slip st to first sc, finish off.

Design by Mary Beth Temple.

If you slow down to take crochet and life a stitch at a time, you will find that there will be much less ripping back...

Buttoned Up

EASY

Finished Size: 16" high x 20" wide (40.5 cm x 51 cm)

SHOPPING LIST

Yarn (Medium Weight) MEDIUM 4
[4 ounces, 186 yards (113 grams, 170 meters) per skein]:
- ☐ Green - 2 skeins
- ☐ Ecru - 1 skein

Crochet Hook
- ☐ Size I (5.5 mm) **or** size needed for gauge

Additional Supplies
- ☐ 16" x 20" (40.5 cm x 51 cm) pillow form
- ☐ 13/16" (30 mm) buttons - 5
- ☐ 7/8" (22 mm) buttons - 5
- ☐ Tapestry needle

GAUGE INFORMATION

In pattern, 5 3-sc groups and 13 rows = 3¾" (9.5 cm)

Gauge Swatch: 3¾" (9.5 cm) square

With Green, ch 15.

Row 1: 3 Sc in third ch from hook, (skip next 2 chs, 3 sc in next ch) across: 5 3-sc groups.

Rows 2-13: Ch 1, turn; skip first sc, 3 sc in next sc, (skip next 2 sc, 3 sc in next sc) across to last sc, leave last sc unworked. Finish off.

BODY (Make 2)

With Ecru ch 27, drop Ecru, with Green ch 54: 81 chs.

Row 1 (Right side)**:** 3 Sc in third ch from hook, (skip next 2 chs, 3 sc in next ch) 17 times changing to Ecru in last sc made ***(Fig. 7b, page 124)***, (skip next 2 chs, 3 sc in next ch) across: 27 3-sc groups (18 Green and 9 Ecru).

Note: Loop a short piece of yarn around any stitch to mark Row 1 as **right** side.

Row 2: Ch 1, turn; skip first sc, 3 sc in next sc, (skip next 2 sc, 3 sc in next sc) 8 times changing to Green in last sc made, (skip next 2 sc, 3 sc in next sc) across to last sc, leave last sc unworked.

Row 3: Ch 1 turn; skip first sc, 3 sc in next sc, (skip next 2 sc, 3 sc in next sc) 17 times changing to Ecru in last sc made, (skip next 2 sc, 3 sc in next sc) across to last sc, leave last sc unworked.

Repeat Rows 2 and 3 for pattern until piece measures approximately 16" (40.5 cm) from beginning ch, ending by working Row 3; finish off Ecru and cut Green.

ACCENT LINE

With **right** side of Body facing and working in sts along color change, insert hook in first st at beginning ch from **front** to **back**, holding Green on **wrong** side, YO and pull up a loop, ★ insert hook in st on next row, YO and draw through st **and** loop on hook; repeat from ★ across; finish off.

FINISHING

Stack one smaller button on top of one larger button, lining up holes. Using photo as a guide for placement, sew stacked button to Accent Line using 3 strands of Green. Tie strands in a knot; cut ends and fray.

Repeat with remaining buttons, this will be the front.

EDGING

Rnd 1 (Joining rnd)**:** With **wrong** sides of Body pieces together, matching colors and front facing, join Ecru with sc in first st on Ecru section ***(see Joining With Sc, page 123)***; working through **both** layers; sc in each st across to next corner, 3 sc in corner; working in end of rows, sc evenly across to next corner, 3 sc in corner, sc in each st across to color change changing to Green in last sc made, sc in each sc across to next corner, 3 sc in corner, insert pillow form; working in end of rows, sc evenly across to next corner, 3 sc in corner; sc in each st across; join with slip st to first sc.

Rnd 2: Ch 1, working from **left** to **right**, work reverse sc in same st ***(Figs. 10a-d, page 125)*** and in each sc around to color change changing to Ecru in last sc made, cut Green; work reverse sc in next sc and in each sc around; join with slip st to first st, finish off.

Design by Mary Beth Temple.

Cushy Pillow

EASY

Finished Size: 10" x 16"
(25.5 cm x 40.5 cm)

SHOPPING LIST

Yarn (Medium Weight) 4

[3 ounces, 197 yards
(85 grams, 180 meters) per skein]:

- ☐ Brown - 2 skeins
- ☐ Ecru Fleck - 1 skein
- ☐ Ecru - 1 skein
- ☐ Pink - 1 skein
- ☐ Rose - 1 skein

Crochet Hook

- ☐ Size I (5.5 mm)
  or size needed for gauge

Additional Supplies

- ☐ 10" x 16" (25.5 cm x 40.5 cm) pillow form

GAUGE INFORMATION

12 linked dc and 7 rows = 4" (10 cm)

Gauge Swatch: 4" (10 cm) square

Ch 14.

Rows 1-7: Work same as Back: 12 linked dc.

Finish off.

STITCH GUIDE

BEGINNING LINKED DOUBLE CROCHET
(abbreviated beginning linked dc)

Insert hook in second ch from hook, YO and pull up a loop, insert hook in first linked dc, YO and pull up a loop (3 loops on hook), (YO and draw through 2 loops on hook) twice.

LINKED DOUBLE CROCHET
(abbreviated linked dc)

Insert hook in horizontal bar of previous linked dc ***(Fig. A)***, YO and pull up a loop, insert hook in next st, YO and pull up a loop (3 loops on hook) ***(Fig. B)***, (YO and draw through 2 loops on hook) twice ***(Fig. C)***.

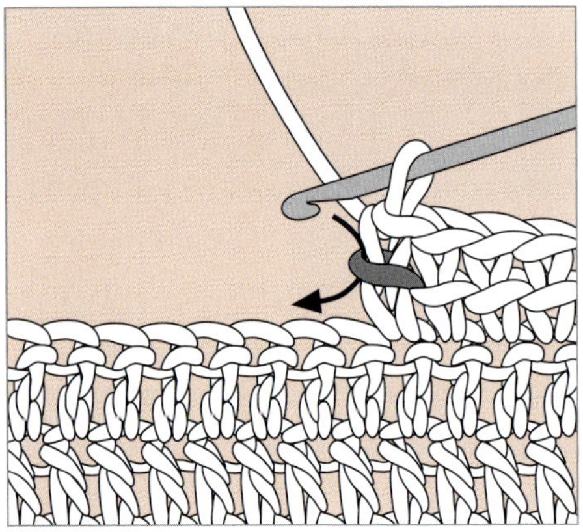

Fig. A

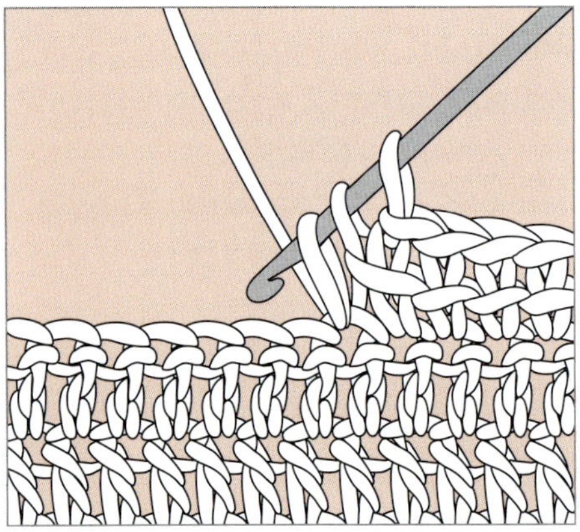

Fig. B

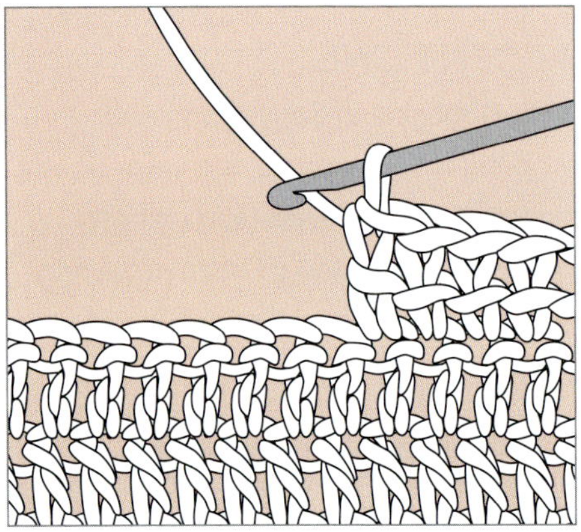

Fig. C

BACK

With Brown, ch 31, place marker in third ch from hook for st placement.

Row 1 (Right side)**:** Insert hook in second ch from hook, YO and pull up a loop, insert hook in marked ch, do **not** remove marker, YO and pull up a loop (3 loops on hook), (YO and draw through 2 loops on hook) twice **(counts as first linked dc)**, work linked dc across: 29 linked dc.

Note: Loop a short piece of yarn around any stitch to mark Row 1 as **right** side.

Rows 2-29: Ch 2, turn; work beginning linked dc, work linked dc across.

Do **not** finish off.

TRIM

Ch 1, do **not** turn; work 46 sc evenly spaced across ends of rows; working in free loops of beginning ch ***(Fig. 5b, page 124)***, 3 sc in first ch, sc in each ch across to marked ch, 3 sc in marked ch, remove marker; work 46 sc evenly spaced across ends of rows; 3 sc in first linked dc, sc in each linked dc across to last linked dc, 3 sc in last linked dc; join with slip st to first sc, finish off: 158 sc.

FRONT

With Brown, ch 31, place marker in third ch from hook for st placement.

Rows 1-8: Work same as Back: 29 linked dc.

Row 9: Ch 2, turn; work beginning linked dc, work linked dc across changing to Ecru Fleck in last linked dc ***(Fig. 7d, page 124)***, cut Brown.

Rows 10-13: Ch 2, turn; work beginning linked dc, work linked dc across.

Row 14: Ch 2, turn; work beginning linked dc, work linked dc across changing to Ecru in last linked dc, cut Ecru Fleck.

Rows 15-19: Repeat Rows 10-14 changing to Pink in last linked dc, cut Ecru.

Rows 20-24: Repeat Rows 10-14 changing to Rose in last linked dc, cut Pink.

Rows 25-29: Repeat Rows 10-14 changing to Brown in last linked dc, cut Rose.

TRIM

Work same as Back.

FINISHING

With **wrong** sides together, Front facing, and working through inside loops only of **both** pieces, join Brown with sc in any sc ***(see Joining With Sc, page 123)***; sc in each sc around, inserting pillow form before closing; join with slip st to **both** loops of first sc, finish off.

Design by Kristi Simpson.

Plush Pillow

EASY

Finished Size: 18½" wide x 16" high (47 cm x 40.5 cm)

SHOPPING LIST

Yarn (Medium Weight) 4

[4 ounces, 212 yards (113 grams, 194 meters) per skein]:

☐ 4 skeins

Crochet Hook

☐ Size I (5.5 mm) **or** size needed for gauge

Additional Supplies

☐ 18½" x 16" (47 cm x 40.5 cm) pillow form **or** 20" x 33" (51 cm x 84 cm) fabric and polyester fiberfill

☐ Yarn needle

GAUGE INFORMATION

In Crocodile Stitch,
3 Scales and 10 rows = 4" (10 cm)
In Back pattern,
11 dc and 7 rows = 3½" (9 cm)

Gauge Swatch: 3½" (9 cm) square

Ch 13.

Row 1: Dc in fourth ch from hook (**3 skipped chs count as first dc**) and in each ch across: 11 dc.

Rows 2-7: Ch 3 (**counts as first dc**), turn; dc in next dc and in each dc across. Finish off.

FRONT

Ch 82.

Row 1 (Foundation row - Wrong side row)**:** Dc in fourth ch from hook (**3 skipped chs count as first dc**), ★ ch 1, skip next 2 chs, dc in next ch, ch 1, skip next 2 chs, 2 dc in next ch; repeat from ★ across: 14 2-dc groups, 13 dc, and 26 chs.

Row 2 (Scale row)**:** Ch 1, work 5 dc down post of last dc made working over beginning end ***(Fig. A)***, ch 1, rotate Foundation Row and work 5 dc up post of next dc to form a Scale ***(Figs. B & C)***, ★ skip next ch, slip st in next dc, skip next ch, work 5 dc down post of next dc, ch 1, rotate piece and work 5 dc up post of next dc; repeat from ★ across, slip st around post of same dc: 14 Scales.

Fig. A

Fig. B

Fig. C

Row 3 (Foundation row)**:** Ch 4 **(counts as first dc plus ch 1, now and throughout)**, 2 dc in next slip st (between Scales) ***(Fig. D)***, ch 1, dc in center of next Scale ***(Fig. E)***, ★ ch 1, 2 dc in next slip st, ch 1, dc in center of next Scale; repeat from ★ across: 13 2-dc groups, 14 dc, and 26 chs.

Row 4 (Scale row)**:** Turn; slip st in first dc, ★ skip next ch, work 5 dc down post of next dc, ch 1, rotate piece and work 5 dc up post of next dc, skip next ch, slip st in next dc; repeat from ★ across: 13 Scales.

Row 5 (Foundation row)**:** Ch 3 **(counts as first dc, now and throughout)**, turn; dc in first slip st, ★ ch 1, dc in center of next Scale, ch 1, 2 dc in next slip st; repeat from ★ across: 14 2-dc groups, 13 dc, and 26 chs.

Row 6 (Scale row)**:** Ch 1, work 5 dc down post of last dc made, ch 1, rotate piece and work 5 dc up post of next dc to form a Scale, ★ skip next ch, slip st in next dc, skip next ch, work 5 dc down post of next dc, ch 1, rotate piece and work 5 dc up post of next dc; repeat from ★ across, slip st around post of same dc: 14 Scales.

Repeat Rows 3-6 for pattern until Front measures approximately 16" (40.5 cm) from beginning ch, ending by working Row 6; do **not** finish off.

BACK

Row 1: Ch 1, turn; 3 sc in center of first Scale, 3 sc in next slip st, 2 sc in center of next Scale, (2 sc in next slip st, 2 sc in center of next Scale) across to last slip st, 3 sc in last slip st, 3 sc in center of last Scale: 58 sc.

Fig. D

Fig. E

Row 2: Ch 3, turn; dc in next st and in each st across.

Repeat Row 2 until Back measures same as Front; finish off.

If desired, using piece as a guide, make a pillow form or cover a purchased pillow form.

With **wrong** side together, whipstitch across 2 sides ***(Figs. 12a & b, page 126)***; insert pillow form and whipstitch across remaining side.

Design by Lisa Gentry.

There's no scary way to say —
Popcorns,
Bobbles,
or Puffs.
But Crocodile? — ask
Captain Hook about that one!

Undulations Pillow

EASY

Finished Size: 12" (30.5 cm) square

SHOPPING LIST

Yarn (Medium Weight) MEDIUM 4

[3 ounces, 145 yards
(85 grams, 133 meters) per skein]:
- ☐ Beige - 1 skein

[3.5 ounces, 170 yards
(100 grams, 156 meters) per skein]:
- ☐ Brown - 1 skein
- ☐ Taupe - 1 skein
- ☐ Gray - 1 skein

Crochet Hook
- ☐ Size J (6 mm)
  or size needed for gauge

Additional Supplies
- ☐ 7/8" (22 mm) buttons - 4
- ☐ 12" (30.5 cm) square covered pillow form (to coordinate with Beige and Brown)
- ☐ Yarn needle

GAUGE INFORMATION

12 dc and 7 rows = 4" (10 cm)

Gauge Swatch: 4" (10 cm) square

Row 1: With Beige, work 12 foundation dc.

Rows 2-7: Ch 2 (does **not** count as a st), turn; dc in first dc and in each dc across. Finish off.

STITCH GUIDE

FOUNDATION DOUBLE CROCHET
(abbreviated foundation dc)

To begin, ch 4, YO, insert hook in fourth ch from hook **(3 skipped chs count as first foundation dc)**, YO and pull up a loop, YO and draw through one loop on hook **(ch 1 made)**, (YO and draw through 2 loops on hook) twice **(foundation dc made)**.

To work each additional foundation dc, YO, insert hook in ch at base of dc just made, YO and pull up a loop, YO and draw through one loop on hook **(ch 1 made)**, (YO and draw through 2 loops on hook) twice **(foundation dc made,** ***Fig. A*****)**.

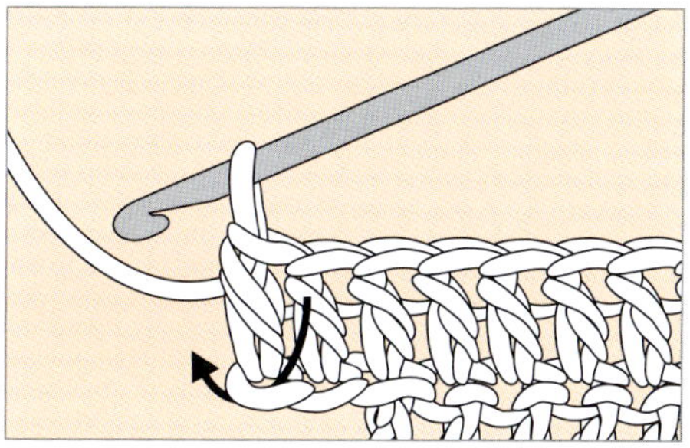

Fig. A

DOUBLE TREBLE CROCHET
(abbreviated dtr)

YO 3 times, insert hook in st indicated, YO and pull up a loop (5 loops on hook), (YO and draw through 2 loops on hook) 4 times.

3-DC POPCORN (uses one sc)

Work 3 dc in sc indicated, drop loop from hook, insert hook from **front** to **back** in first dc of 3-dc group, hook dropped loop and draw through st.

BACK

Row 1 (Right side)**:** With Beige, work 35 foundation dc.

Note: Loop a short piece of yarn around any stitch to mark Row 1 as **right** side.

Rows 2-20: Ch 2 (**does not count as a st, now and throughout Back and Front**), turn; dc in first dc and in each dc across.

Finish off.

FRONT

Row 1 (Right side)**:** With Brown, work 35 foundation dc.

Note: Mark Row 1 as **right** side.

Row 2: Ch 2, turn; dc in Front Loop Only of first dc and each dc across ***(Fig. 4, page 124)***.

Row 3: Ch 2, turn; dc in Back Loop Only of first dc and in each dc across.

Rows 4-7: Repeat Rows 2 and 3 twice.

Finish off.

Row 8: With **wrong** side facing and working in both loops, join Beige with slip st in first dc; ch 2, dc in same st and in each dc across.

Rows 9-11: Ch 2, turn; dc in first dc and in each dc across.

Finish off.

Row 12: With **wrong** side facing, join Gray with slip st in first dc; ch 2, dc in same st and in each dc across.

Rows 13-19: Ch 2, turn; dc in first dc and in each dc across.

Finish off.

RUFFLES

With **right** side facing and working in free loops of Row 1 ***(Fig. 5a, page 124)***, join Brown with slip st in first dc; (ch 3, slip st in next dc) across; finish off.

Work Ruffle on Rows 2, 4, and 5.

ORGANIC SHAPES

SHAPE 1

With Gray, ch 9; join with slip st to form a ring.

Rnd 1 (Right side)**:** Ch 5, 17 dtr in ring; join with slip st to top of beginning ch-5: 18 sts.

Note: Mark Rnd 1 as **right** side.

Rnd 2: Ch 1, sc in same st as joining and in each dtr around; join with slip st to first sc; finish off leaving a long end for sewing.

Rnd 3: With **right** side facing, join Beige with slip st in first sc; ch 3, dc in same st as joining, 2 dc in next sc and in each sc around; join with slip st to top of beginning ch-3, finish off: 36 sts.

Rnd 4: With **right** side facing, join Taupe with slip st in first st; ch 2 (**counts as first hdc**), hdc in same st, 2 hdc in next dc and in each dc around; join with slip st to first hdc, finish off.

SHAPE 2

With Gray, ch 6; join with slip st to form a ring.

Rnd 1 (Right side)**:** Ch 3, work 11 dc in ring; join with slip st to top of beginning ch-3, finish off: 12 sts.

Note: Mark Rnd 1 as **right** side.

Rnd 2: With **right** side facing, join Beige with slip st in same st as joining; ch 5, 2 dtr in same st, 3 dtr in next dc and in each dc around; join with slip st to top of beginning ch-5, finish off leaving a long end for sewing: 36 sts.

Rnd 3: With **right** side facing, join Gray with slip st in same st as joining; ch 1, working from **left** to **right**, work reverse sc in each dtr around ***(Figs. 10a-d, page 125)***; join with slip st to first slip st, finish off.

SHAPE 3

Rnd 1 (Right side)**:** With Taupe and leaving a long end for sewing, ch 4, 11 dc in fourth ch from hook; do **not** join: 12 sts.

Note: Mark Rnd 1 as **right** side.

Rnd 2: Skip next ch of beginning ch-4 and dc in back ridge of next 2 chs ***(Fig. 2, page 124)***, 2 dc in Back Loop Only of next 11 dc; finish off: 24 dc.

Trim: With **right** side facing and working in free loops on Rnd 1, join Beige with slip st in first st (at center of spiral); ch 1, sc in same st and in each dc around; sc in both loops of each dc on Rnd 2 forming a spiral; finish off.

4

5

SHAPE 4

Rnd 1 (Right side)**:** With Taupe, ch 4, 11 dc in fourth ch from hook; join with slip st to top of beginning ch-4, finish off: 12 sts.

Note: Mark Rnd 1 as **right** side.

Rnd 2: With **right** side facing and leaving a long end for sewing, join Gray with slip st in same st as joining; ch 3, dc in same st, 2 dc in next dc and in each dc around; join with slip st to top of beginning ch-3, finish off: 24 sts.

Rnd 3: With **right** side facing, join Brown with slip st in same st as joining; ch 3, slip st in same st, (slip st, ch 3, slip st) in next dc and in each dc around; join with slip st to first slip st, finish off.

SHAPE 5

With Beige, ch 9; join with slip st to form a ring.

Rnd 1 (Right side)**:** Ch 1, 13 sc in ring; join with slip st to first sc, finish off.

Note: Mark Rnd 1 as **right** side.

Rnd 2: With **right** side facing and leaving a long end for sewing, join Taupe with slip st in same st as joining; ch 3, work 3-dc Popcorn in same sc, ch 2, (work 3-dc Popcorn in next sc, ch 2) around; join with slip st to top of first Popcorn, finish off: 13 Popcorns and 13 ch-2 sps.

FINISHING

Using diagram as a guide, sew Organic Shapes to Front using long ends.

JOINING

The Back is one row longer than the Front to allow for an overlap when buttoned. When joining pieces, leave the last row of the Back unjoined.

Hold **wrong** sides of Front and Back together with Front facing. Working through **both** layers and in ends of rows along left edge, join Brown with slip st in Row 19; ch 1, sc evenly across; working in ch at base of each foundation dc, 3 sc in first ch, sc in each ch across to last ch, 3 sc in last ch; sc evenly across ends of rows leaving Row 20 of Back unworked; working across Row 19 of **Front only**, 3 sc in first dc, sc in next 4 dc, ch 3 (**button loop made**), sc in next 8 dc, ch 3, sc in next 9 dc, ch 3, sc in next 8 dc, ch 3, sc in next 4 dc, 3 sc in last dc; join with slip st to first sc, finish off.

EDGING

With Front facing, join Taupe with slip st in same st as joining; ch 1, working from **left** to **right**, work reverse sc in same st and in next 7 sc, working **behind** button loop, work reverse sc in next 2 dc on Row 19 (between button loop), continue to work reverse sc across Front in same manner and in each sc around remaining 3 sides; join with slip st to first st, finish off.

Sew buttons to Back at top of Row 19 to correspond with button loops.

Insert pillow form.

Design by Sheryl Means.

Pouf

EASY

Finished Size:
Approximately 65" diameter x 13" high (165 cm x 33 cm)

SHOPPING LIST

Yarn (Medium Weight) 4
[1.75 ounces, 80 yards (50 grams, 73 meters) per skein]:
- ☐ Cream - 4 skeins
- ☐ Violet - 3 skeins
- ☐ Dk Violet - 3 skeins
- ☐ Tan - 3 skeins

Crochet Hook
- ☐ Size H (5 mm) **or** size needed for gauge

Additional Supplies
- ☐ Polyester fiberfill - 50 ounces (1,420 grams)
- ☐ Safety pin
- ☐ Yarn needle

GAUGE INFORMATION

Gauge Swatch: 4" (10 cm) diameter
Work same as Pouf through Rnd 4: 48 sts.

STITCH GUIDE

SINGLE CROCHET 2 TOGETHER ***(abbreviated sc2tog)***
Pull up a loop in next 2 sts, YO and draw through all 3 loops on hook **(counts as one sc)**.

DOUBLE CROCHET 2 TOGETHER ***(abbreviated dc2tog)*** (uses next 2 sts)
★ YO, insert hook in **next** st, YO and pull up a loop, YO and draw through 2 loops on hook; repeat from ★ once **more**, YO and draw through all 3 loops on hook **(counts as one dc)**.

SPLIT FRONT POST TREBLE CROCHET ***(abbreviated split FPtr)*** (uses 2 FPtr)
YO twice, insert hook from **front** to **back** around post of FPtr **below** next dc ***(Fig. 6, page 124)***, YO and pull up a loop (4 loops on hook), (YO and draw through 2 loops on hook) twice (2 loops on hook), YO twice, insert hook from **front** to **back** around post of **next** FPtr, YO and pull up a loop, (YO and draw through 2 loops on hook) twice, YO and draw through all 3 loops on hook **(counts as one st)**.

CROSS ST (uses one split FPtr)
Skip first leg of split FPtr **below** next dc, work FPtr around next leg, working in **front** of FPtr just made, work FPtr around skipped leg. Skip dc **behind** Cross St.

FRONT POST TREBLE CROCHET ***(abbreviated FPtr)***
YO twice, insert hook from **front** to **back** around post of st indicated ***(Fig. 6, page 124)***, YO and pull up a loop (4 loops on hook), (YO and draw through 2 loops on hook) 3 times. Skip dc **behind** FPtr.

FRONT POST DOUBLE CROCHET ***(abbreviated FPdc)***
YO, insert hook from **front** to **back** around post of st indicated ***(Fig. 6, page 124)***, YO and pull up a loop (3 loops on hook), (YO and draw through 2 loops on hook) twice. Skip dc **behind** FPdc.

POUF

Rnd 1 (Right side)**:** With Dk Violet, ch 4, 11 dc in fourth ch from hook **(3 skipped chs count as first dc)**; join with slip st to first dc changing to Cream ***(Fig. 7a, page 124)***, cut Dk Violet: 12 dc.

Note: Loop a short piece of yarn around any stitch to mark Rnd 1 as **right** side.

Rnd 2: Ch 1, 2 sc in same st as joining, work 2 FPdc around next dc, ★ 2 sc in next dc, work 2 FPdc around next dc; repeat from ★ around; join with slip st to first sc changing to Violet, cut Cream: 24 sts.

Rnd 3: Ch 3 **(counts as first dc, now and throughout)**, 2 dc in next sc, (dc in next st, 2 dc in next st) around; join with slip st to first dc, finish off: 36 dc.

Rnd 4: With **right** side facing, skip first dc and join Cream with sc in next dc ***(see Joining With Sc, page 123)***; 2 sc in next dc, work FPtr around FPdc **below** next dc, ★ sc in next dc, 2 dc in next dc, work FPtr around FPdc **below** next dc; repeat from ★ around; join with slip st to first sc changing to Tan, cut Cream: 48 sts.

Rnd 5: Ch 3, dc in next 2 sc, 2 dc in next FPtr, (dc in next 3 sc, 2 dc in next FPtr) around; join with slip st to first dc changing to Cream, cut Tan: 60 dc.

Rnd 6: Ch 1, sc in same st as joining, ★ † work 2 FPdc around sc **below** next dc, sc in next dc, work FPtr around FPtr **below** next dc, sc in next 4 dc, work FPtr around FPtr **below** next dc †, sc in next dc; repeat from ★ 4 times **more**, then repeat from † to † once; join with slip st to first sc changing to Dk Violet, cut Cream: 12 FPdc, 12 FPtr, and 36 sc.

Rnd 7: Ch 3, dc in next st and in each st around; join with slip st to first dc, finish off.

Rnd 8: With **right** side facing, skip first 2 dc and join Cream with sc in next dc; ★ † work FPtr around FPdc **below** next dc, sc in next 2 dc, work FPtr around FPtr **below** next dc, sc in next dc, work FPtr around FPtr **below** next dc, sc in next 2 dc, work FPtr around FPdc **below** next dc †, sc in next dc; repeat from ★ 4 times **more**, then repeat from † to † once; join with slip st to first sc changing to Violet, cut Cream.

Rnd 9: Ch 3, dc in next 3 sts, 2 dc in next st, (dc in next 4 sts, 2 dc in next st) around; join with slip st to first dc, finish off: 72 dc.

Rnd 10: With **right** side facing, skip first 3 dc and join Cream with sc in next dc; sc in next 3 dc, ★ † work split FPtr, do **not** skip dc behind split FPtr, sc in next 4 dc, work FPtr around FPtr **below** next dc, sc in next 2 dc, work FPtr around FPtr **below** next dc †, sc in next 4 dc; repeat from ★ 4 times **more**, then repeat from † to † once; join with slip st to first sc changing to Tan, cut Cream: 78 sts.

Rnd 11: Ch 3, dc in next sc and in each st around; join with slip st to first dc, finish off.

Rnd 12: With **right** side facing, skip first dc and join Cream with sc in next dc; sc in next 2 dc, ★ † work Cross St, sc in next 4 dc, work FPtr around FPtr **below** next dc, sc in next 3 dc, work FPtr around FPtr **below** next dc †, sc in next 3 dc; repeat from ★ 4 times **more**, then repeat from † to † once; join with slip st to first sc changing to Dk Violet, cut Cream: 84 sts.

Rnd 13: Ch 3, dc in next 4 sts, 2 dc in next st, (dc in next 13 sts, 2 dc in next st) around to last 9 sts, dc in last 9 sts; join with slip st to first dc changing to Cream, cut Dk Violet: 90 dc.

Rnd 14: Ch 1, sc in same st as joining and in next 2 dc, ★ † work FPtr around next FPtr **below** next dc, sc in next 2 dc, work FPtr around next FPtr **below** next dc, sc in next 5 dc, work FPtr around next 2 FPtr **below** next 2 dc †, sc in next 4 dc; repeat from ★ 4 times **more**, repeat from † to † once, sc in last dc; join with slip st to first sc, finish off: 24 FPtr and 66 sc.

Rnd 15: With **right** side facing, join Violet with dc in last sc made; dc in next 13 sts, 2 dc in next st, (dc in next 14 sts, 2 dc in next st) around; join with slip st to first dc changing to Cream, cut Violet: 96 dc.

Rnd 16: Ch 1, sc in same st as joining and in next 5 dc, ★ † work split FPtr, skip dc **behind** split FPtr, sc in next 7 dc, skip next FPtr **below** next dc, work FPtr around next FPtr, working in **front** of FPtr just made, work FPtr around skipped FPtr †, sc in next 6 dc; repeat from ★ 4 times **more**, then repeat from † to † once; join with slip st to first sc changing to Tan, cut Cream: 78 sc, 12 FPtr, and 6 split FPtr.

Rnd 17: Ch 3, dc in next 14 sts, 2 dc in next st, (dc in next 15 sts, 2 dc in next st) around; join with slip st to first dc, finish off: 102 dc.

Rnd 18: With **right** side facing, skip first dc and join Cream with sc in next dc; sc in next dc, ★ † 2 sc in next dc, sc in next 2 dc, work FPtr around split FPtr **below** next dc, sc in next 7 dc, work FPtr around next FPtr **below** next dc, sc in next 2 dc, work FPtr around next FPtr **below** next dc †, sc in next 2 dc; repeat from ★ 4 times **more**, then repeat from † to † once; join with slip st to first sc changing to Dk Violet, cut Cream: 108 sts.

Rnd 19: Ch 3, dc in next 2 sc, 2 dc in next sc, dc in next 6 sts, 2 dc in next st, ★ dc in next 10 sts, 2 dc in next st, dc in next 6 sts, 2 dc in next st; repeat from ★ around to last 7 sts, dc in last 7 sts; join with slip st to first dc changing to Cream, cut Dk Violet: 120 dc.

Rnd 20: Ch 1, sc in same st as joining and in next 4 dc, ★ † 2 sc in next dc, sc in next 7 dc, 2 sc in next dc, sc in next 5 dc, work split FPtr, skip dc **behind** split FPtr †, sc in next 5 dc; repeat from ★ 4 times **more**, then repeat from † to † once; join with slip st to first sc changing to Violet, cut Cream: 132 sts.

Rnd 21: Ch 3, dc in next 5 sts, 2 dc in next st, dc in next 8 sts, 2 dc in next st, ★ dc in next 12 sts, 2 dc in next st, dc in next 8 sts, 2 dc in next st; repeat from ★ around to last 6 sts, dc in last 6 sts; join with slip st to first dc changing to Cream, cut Violet: 144 dc.

Rnd 22: Ch 1, sc in same st as joining and in next 6 dc, ★ † 2 sc in next dc, sc in next 9 dc, 2 sc in next dc, sc in next 5 dc, work FPtr around split FPtr **below** next dc †, sc in next 7 dc; repeat from ★ 4 times **more**, then repeat from † to † once; join with slip st to first sc changing to Tan, cut Cream: 156 sts.

Rnd 23: Ch 3, dc in next 24 sts, 2 dc in next st, (dc in next 25 sts, 2 dc in next st) around; join with slip st to first dc changing to Cream, cut Tan: 162 dc.

Rnd 24: Ch 1, sc in same st as joining and in next 25 dc, 2 sc in next dc, (sc in next 26 dc, 2 sc in next dc) around; join with slip st to first sc changing to Dk Violet, cut Cream: 168 sc.

Rnd 25: Ch 3, dc in next 26 sc, 2 dc in next sc, (dc in next 27 sc, 2 dc in next sc) around; join with slip st to first dc changing to Cream, cut Dk Violet: 174 dc.

Rnd 26: Ch 1, sc in same st as joining and in each dc around; join with slip st to first sc changing to Violet, cut Cream.

Rnd 27: Ch 3, dc in next sc and in each sc around; join with slip st to first dc changing to Cream, cut Violet.

Rnd 28: Ch 1, sc in same st as joining and in each dc around; join with slip st to first sc changing to Tan, cut Cream.

Rnd 29: Ch 3, dc in next sc and in each sc around; join with slip st to first dc changing to Cream, cut Tan.

Rnd 30: Ch 1, sc in same st as joining and in next 2 dc, work FPtr around sc **below** next dc, ★ sc in next 5 dc, work FPtr around sc **below** next dc; repeat from ★ around to last 2 dc, sc in last 2 dc; join with slip st to first sc changing to Dk Violet, cut Cream.

Rnd 31: Ch 3, dc in next sc and in each st around; join with slip st to first dc changing to Cream, cut Dk Violet.

Rnd 32: Ch 1, sc in same st as joining, ★ † work FPtr around next FPtr **below** next dc, sc in next 3 dc, work FPtr **below** same FPtr as last FPtr made †, sc in next dc; repeat from ★ around to last 5 sts, then repeat from † to † once; join with slip st to first sc changing to Violet, cut Cream.

Rnd 33: Ch 3, dc in next st and in each st around; join with slip st to first dc changing to Cream, cut Violet.

Rnd 34: Ch 1, sc in same st as joining and in next 2 dc, work split FPtr, skip dc **behind** split FPtr, ★ sc in next 5 dc, work split FPtr, skip dc **behind** split FPtr; repeat from ★ around to last 2 dc, sc in last 2 sc; join with slip st to first sc changing to Tan, cut Cream.

Rnd 35: Ch 3, dc in next st and in each st around; join with slip st to first dc, finish off.

Rnd 36: With **right** side facing, skip first dc and join Cream with sc in next dc; sc in next dc, ★ † work FPtr around next split FPtr, sc in next 2 dc, work FPtr around sc **below** next dc †, sc in next 2 dc; repeat from ★ around to last 4 dc, then repeat from † to † once; join with slip st to first sc changing to Dk Violet, cut Cream.

Rnd 37: Ch 3, dc in next sc and in each st around; join with slip st to first dc, finish off.

Rnd 38: With **right** side facing, skip first 2 dc and join Cream with sc in next dc; ★ † work FPtr around next FPtr, sc in next 3 dc, work FPtr **below** same FPtr as last FPtr made †, sc in next dc; repeat from ★ around to last 5 dc, then repeat from † to † once; join with slip st to first sc changing to Violet, cut Cream.

Rnds 39-47: Repeat Rnds 33-38 once, then repeat Rnds 33-35 once **more**.

Rnd 48: With **right** side facing, skip first 4 dc and join Cream with sc in next dc; sc in next 4 dc, work FPtr around next split FPtr, ★ sc in next 5 dc, work FPtr around next split FPtr; repeat from ★ around; join with slip st to first sc changing to Dk Violet, cut Cream.

Rnd 49: Ch 3, dc in next sc and in each st around; join with slip st to first dc changing to Cream, cut Dk Violet.

Rnds 50-52: Repeat Rnds 26-28.

Rnd 53: Ch 3, dc in next 26 sc, dc2tog, (dc in next 27 sc, dc2tog) around; join with slip st to first dc changing to Cream, cut Tan: 168 dc.

Rnd 54: Ch 1, sc in same st as joining and in next 25 dc, sc2tog, (sc in next 26 dc, sc2tog) around; join with slip st to first sc changing to Dk Violet, cut Cream: 162 sc.

Rnd 55: Ch 3, dc in next 24 sc, dc2tog, (dc in next 25 sc, dc2tog) around; join with slip st to first dc changing to Cream, cut Dk Violet: 156 dc.

Rnd 56: Ch 1, sc in same st as joining and in next 10 dc, sc2tog, (sc in next 11 dc, sc2tog) around; join with slip st to first sc changing to Violet, cut Cream: 144 sc.

Rnd 57: Ch 3, dc in next 9 sc, dc2tog, (dc in next 10 sc, dc2tog) around; join with slip st to first dc changing to Cream, cut Violet: 132 dc.

Rnd 58: Ch 1, sc in same st as joining and in next 8 dc, sc2tog, (sc in next 9 dc, sc2tog) around; join with slip st to first sc changing to Tan, cut Cream: 120 sc.

Rnd 59: Ch 3, dc in next 7 sc, dc2tog, (dc in next 8 sc, dc2tog) around; join with slip st to first dc changing Cream, cut Tan: 108 dc.

Rnd 60: Ch 1, sc in same st as joining and in next 15 dc, sc2tog, (sc in next 16 dc, sc2tog) around; join with slip st to first sc changing to Dk Violet, cut Cream: 102 sc.

Rnd 61: Ch 3, dc in next 14 sc, dc2tog, (dc in next 15 sc, dc2tog) around; join with slip st to first dc changing to Cream, cut Dk Violet: 96 dc.

Rnd 62: Ch 1, sc in same st as joining and in each dc around; join with slip st to first sc changing to Violet, cut Cream.

Rnd 63: Ch 3, dc in next 13 sc, dc2tog, (dc in next 14 sc, dc2tog) around; join with slip st to first dc changing to Cream, cut Violet: 90 dc.

Rnd 64: Ch 1, sc in same st as joining and in each dc around, join with slip st to first sc changing to Tan, cut Cream.

Rnd 65: Ch 3, dc in next 12 sc, dc2tog, (dc in next 13 sc, dc2tog) around; join with slip st to first dc changing to Cream, cut Tan: 84 dc.

Rnd 66: Ch 1, sc in same st as joining and in next 11 dc, sc2tog, (sc in next 12 dc, sc2tog) around; join with slip st to first sc changing to Dk Violet, cut Cream: 78 sc.

Rnd 67: Ch 3, dc in next sc and in each sc around; join with slip st to first dc changing to Cream, cut Dk Violet.

Rnd 68: Ch 1, sc in same st as joining and next 10 dc, sc2tog, (sc in next 11 dc, sc2tog) around; join with slip st to first sc changing to Violet, cut Cream: 72 sc.

Rnd 69: Ch 3, dc in next 3 sc, dc2tog, (dc in next 4 sc, dc2tog) around; join with slip st to first dc changing to Cream, cut Violet, place loop from hook onto safety pin to keep piece from unraveling: 60 dc.

Stuff Pouf firmly with polyester fiberfill.

Rnd 70: Remove loop from safety pin and place on hook; ch 1, sc in same st as joining and in next 2 dc, sc2tog, (sc in next 3 dc, sc2tog) around; join with slip st to first sc changing to Tan, cut Cream: 48 sc.

Rnd 71: Ch 3, dc in next sc, dc2tog, (dc in next 2 sc, dc2tog) around; join with slip st to first dc changing to Cream, cut Tan: 36 dc.

Rnd 72: Ch 1, sc in same st as joining, sc2tog, (sc in next dc, sc2tog) around; join with slip st to first sc changing to Dk Violet, cut Cream: 24 sc.

Rnd 73: Ch 2 **(does not count as a st)**, dc2tog around; join with slip st to first dc changing to Cream, cut Dk Violet: 12 dc.

Rnd 74: Ch 1, sc2tog around; join with slip st to first sc, finish off leaving a long end for sewing: 6 sc.

Thread yarn needle with long end and weave through sts on Rnd 74 to close.

Design by Kristi Simpson.

for your furry friends

Pet Bed

EASY

SHOPPING LIST

Yarn (Medium Weight) 4

[4 ounces, 235 yards
(113 grams, 215 meters) per skein]:

- ☐ Navy - 2 skeins
- ☐ Gray - 1 skein

Crochet Hook

- ☐ Size H (5 mm)
  or size needed for gauge

SIZE INFORMATION

Size: Small{Medium-Large}

Finished Measurements:
10{12-14}" diameter x 3½" high
[25.5{30.5-35.5} cm x 9 cm]

Size Note: We have printed the instructions for the sizes in different colors to make it easier for you to find:

- Size Small in Blue
- Size Medium in Pink
- Size Large in Green

Instructions in Black apply to all sizes.

GAUGE INFORMATION

Holding 2 strands of yarn together,
13 sc and 12 rows/rnds = 4" (10 cm)

Gauge Swatch: 4" (10 cm) square

Holding 2 strands of Navy together, ch 14.

Row 1: Sc in second ch from hook and in each ch across: 13 sc.

Rows 2-12: Ch 1, turn; sc in each sc across.

Finish off.

STITCH GUIDE

BACK POST SINGLE CROCHET
(abbreviated BPsc)
Insert hook from **back** to **front** around post of st indicated *(Fig. 6, page 124)*, YO and pull up a loop, YO and draw through both loops on hook.

LONG SINGLE CROCHET
(abbreviated LSC)
Working **around** previous rnd, insert hook in sc indicated, YO and pull up a loop even with last st made, YO and draw through both loops on hook *(Fig. 11, page 125)*.

Pet Bed is worked holding two strands of yarn together throughout.

BOTTOM

Rnd 1: Holding 2 strands of Navy together, make an adjustable loop to form a ring *(Figs. 1a-d, page 123)*, work 10 sc in ring; join with slip st to first sc.

Rnd 2: Ch 1, 2 sc in each sc around; join with slip st to first sc: 20 sc.

Rnd 3: Ch 1, 2 sc in first sc, sc in next sc, (2 sc in next sc, sc in next sc) around; join with slip st to first sc: 30 sc.

Rnd 4: Ch 1, sc in each sc around; join with slip st to first sc.

Rnd 5: Ch 1, sc in first 2 sc, 2 sc in next sc, (sc in next 2 sc, 2 sc in next sc) around; join with slip st to first sc: 40 sc.

Rnd 6: Ch 1, 2 sc in first sc, sc in next 3 sc, (2 sc in next sc, sc in next 3 sc) around; join with slip st to first sc: 50 sc.

Rnd 7: Ch 1, sc in each sc around; join with slip st to first sc.

Rnd 8: Ch 1, sc in first 4 sc, 2 sc in next sc, (sc in next 4 sc, 2 sc in next sc) around; join with slip st to first sc: 60 sc.

Rnd 9: Ch 1, 2 sc in first sc, sc in next 5 sc, (2 sc in next sc, sc in next 5 sc) around; join with slip st to first sc: 70 sc.

Rnd 10: Ch 1, sc in each sc around; join with slip st to first sc.

Rnd 11: Ch 1, sc in first 6 sc, 2 sc in next sc, (sc in next 6 sc, 2 sc in next sc) around; join with slip st to first sc: 80 sc.

Rnd 12: Ch 1, 2 sc in first sc, sc in next 7 sc, (2 sc in next sc, sc in next 7 sc) around; join with slip st to first sc: 90 sc.

Rnd 13: Ch 1, sc in each sc around; join with slip st to first sc.

Rnd 14: Ch 1, sc in first 8 sc, 2 sc in next sc, (sc in next 8 sc, 2 sc in next sc) around; join with slip st to first sc, do **not** finish off: 100 sc.

Sizes Medium & Large ONLY

Rnd 15: Ch 1, 2 sc in first sc, sc in next 9 sc, (2 sc in next sc, sc in next 9 sc) around; join with slip st to first sc: 110 sc.

Rnd 16: Ch 1, sc in each sc around; join with slip st to first sc.

Rnd 17: Ch 1, sc in first 10 sc, 2 sc in next sc, (sc in next 10 sc, 2 sc in next sc) around; join with slip st to first sc; do **not** finish off: 120 sc.

Size Large ONLY

Rnd 18: Ch 1, 2 sc in first sc, sc in next 11 sc, (2 sc in next sc, sc in next 11 sc) around; join with slip st to first sc: 130 sc.

Rnd 19: Ch 1, sc in each sc around; join with slip st to first sc.

Rnd 20: Ch 1, sc in first 12 sc, 2 sc in next sc, (sc in next 12 sc, 2 sc in next sc) around; join with slip st to first sc, do **not** finish off: 140 sc.

SIDES - ALL SIZES

Rnd 1 (Right side)**:** Ch 1, **turn**; work BPsc around next sc and each sc around; join with slip st to first BPsc: 100{120-140} BPsc.

Rnds 2-4: Ch 1, do **not** turn; sc in each st around; join with slip st to first sc.

Rnd 5: Ch 1, sc in each sc around; cut Navy, holding 2 strands of Gray together, join with slip st to first sc ***(Fig. 7a, page 124)***.

Rnd 6: Ch 1, sc in first 4 sc, work LSC in sc one rnd **below** next sc, ★ sc in next 4 sc, work LSC in sc one rnd **below** next sc; repeat from ★ around; join with slip st to first sc: 20{24-28} LSC and 80{96-112} sc.

Rnds 7-9: Ch 1, sc in each st around; join with slip st to first sc.

Rnd 10: Ch 1, (slip st in next sc, ch 1) around; join with slip st to joining slip st, finish off.

Design by Marly Bird.

Pet Blanket & Toy

EASY

SHOPPING LIST

Yarn (100% Cotton Medium Weight)
[1.75 ounces, 80 yards (50 grams, 73 meters) per skein]:

Blanket
- ☐ Yellow - 4{9} skeins
- ☐ Blue - 3{6} skeins
- ☐ Red - 40 yards (36.5 meters)

Toy Mouse
- ☐ Red - 25 yards (23 meters)
- ☐ Blue - small amount
- ☐ Black - small amount

Crochet Hooks
- ☐ Size G (4 mm) **and**
- ☐ Size I (5.5 mm)

or sizes needed for gauge

Additional Supplies
- ☐ Polyester fiberfill
- ☐ Yarn needle

SIZE INFORMATION

Finished Blanket Sizes:

Small - 21½" x 28½" (54.5 cm x 72.5 cm)

Large - 35" x 42" (89 cm x 106.5 cm)

Size Note: We have printed the instructions for the sizes in different colors to make it easier for you to find:
- Size Small in Blue
- Size Large in Green

Instructions in Black apply to both sizes.

Finished Toy Mouse Size

Approximately 3¾" (9.5 cm) long (not including tail)

GAUGE INFORMATION

Blanket

With larger size hook,
Each Square = 6¾" (17.25 cm)

Gauge Swatch: 3¾" (9.5 cm) square
Work same as Maze Square through Rnd 3: 44 dc.

Toy Mouse

Gauge is not of great importance; the toy can be a little larger or smaller without changing the overall effect. Work should be firm enough so that the stuffing does not show through the stitches.

With smaller size hook, gauge is approximately 4 sc and 4 rows = 1" (2.5 cm).

Blanket

MAZE SQUARE

Make 12{30}.

With larger size hook and Blue, ch 5; join with slip st to form a ring.

Rnd 1 (Right side)**:** Ch 3 **(counts as first dc, now and throughout)**, (2 dc, ch 1, 2 dc) in ring, dc in ring changing to Yellow ***(Fig. 7d, page 124)***, ch 1, (3 dc, ch 1) twice in ring; join with slip st to first dc: 12 dc and 4 ch-1 sps.

Note: Loop a short piece of yarn around any stitch to mark Rnd 1 as **right** side.

Rnd 2: Continuing with Yellow, ch 3, dc in next 2 dc, (2 dc, ch 1, 2 dc) in next ch-1 sp, dc in next 3 dc, (2 dc, ch 1, 2 dc) in next ch-1 sp changing to Blue in last dc made, **[**dc in next 3 dc, (2 dc, ch 1, 2 dc) in next ch-1 sp**]** twice; join with slip st to first dc: 28 dc.

Rnd 3: Continuing with Blue, ch 3, dc in next 4 dc, (2 dc, ch 1, 2 dc) in next corner ch-1 sp, dc in next 7 dc, (2 dc, ch 1, 2 dc) in next corner ch-1 sp, dc in next 2 dc changing to Yellow in last dc made, dc in next 5 dc, (2 dc, ch 1, 2 dc) in next corner ch-1 sp, dc in next 7 dc, (2 dc, ch 1, 2 dc) in next corner ch-1 sp, dc in last 2 dc; join with slip st to first dc: 44 dc.

Rnd 4: Continuing with Yellow, ch 3, dc in next 6 dc, (2 dc, ch 1, 2 dc) in next corner ch-1 sp, dc in next 11 dc, (2 dc, ch 1, 2 dc) in next corner ch-1 sp, dc in next 4 dc changing to Blue in last dc made, dc in next 7 dc, (2 dc, ch 1, 2 dc) in next corner ch-1 sp, dc in next 11 dc, (2 dc, ch 1, 2 dc) in next corner ch-1 sp, dc in last 4 dc; join with slip st to first dc: 60 dc.

Rnd 5: Continuing with Blue, ch 3, dc in next 8 dc, (2 dc, ch 1, 2 dc) in next corner ch-1 sp, dc in next 15 dc, (2 dc, ch 1, 2 dc) in next corner ch-1 sp, dc in next 6 dc changing to Yellow in last dc made, cut Blue, dc in next 9 dc, (2 dc, ch 1, 2 dc) in next corner ch-1 sp, dc in next 15 dc, (2 dc, ch 1, 2 dc) in next corner ch-1 sp, dc in last 6 dc; join with slip st to first dc: 76 dc.

Rnd 6: Ch 3, dc in next dc and in each dc around, working (2 dc, ch 1, 2 dc) in each corner ch-1 sp; join with slip st to first dc, finish off: 92 dc.

ASSEMBLY

With Yellow and working through **inside** loops only, whipstitch Squares together *(Fig. 12b, page 126)*, forming 3{5} strips of 4{6} Squares, positioning each Square in same direction and beginning in first corner ch and ending in next corner ch; then whipstitch strips together in same manner.

EDGING

Rnd 1: With **right** side facing and using larger size hook, join Blue with dc in any dc *(see Joining With Dc, page 123)*; dc in next dc and in each dc and each joined corner ch around, working (2 dc, ch 1, 2 dc) in each corner ch-1 sp; join with slip st to first dc, finish off: 358{558} dc and 4 chs.

Rnd 2: With **right** side facing and using larger size hook, join Red with sc in any corner ch *(see Joining With Sc, page 123)*; ch 3, skip next st, ★ sc in next st, ch 3, skip next st; repeat from ★ around; join with slip st to first sc, finish off.

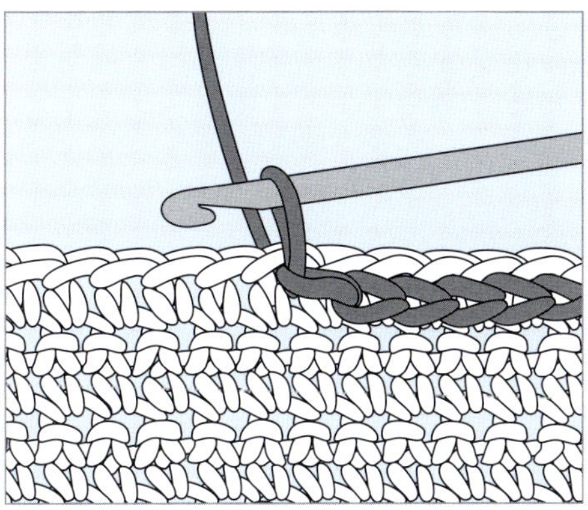

Fig. A

Trim: With **right** side facing, using larger size hook, and working in sts on Rnd 1, insert hook in any dc from **front** to **back**, holding Yellow on **wrong** side, YO and pull up a loop, ★ insert hook in next st, YO and draw through st and loop on hook *(Fig. A)*; repeat from ★ around for surface slip st ending by working in same st as beginning slip st; cut yarn leaving a long end.

Pull the loop on hook allowing the yarn end to come through the last stitch. Thread the yarn needle with the end and insert it under the 2 strands of the first slip st, then down at the same place where yarn emerges, creating a seamless chain; secure end.

Toy Mouse

Use smaller size hook for entire Mouse.

STITCH GUIDE

SINGLE CROCHET 2 TOGETHER
(abbreviated sc2tog)

Pull up a loop in each of next 2 sc, YO and draw through all 3 loops on hook **(counts as one sc)**.

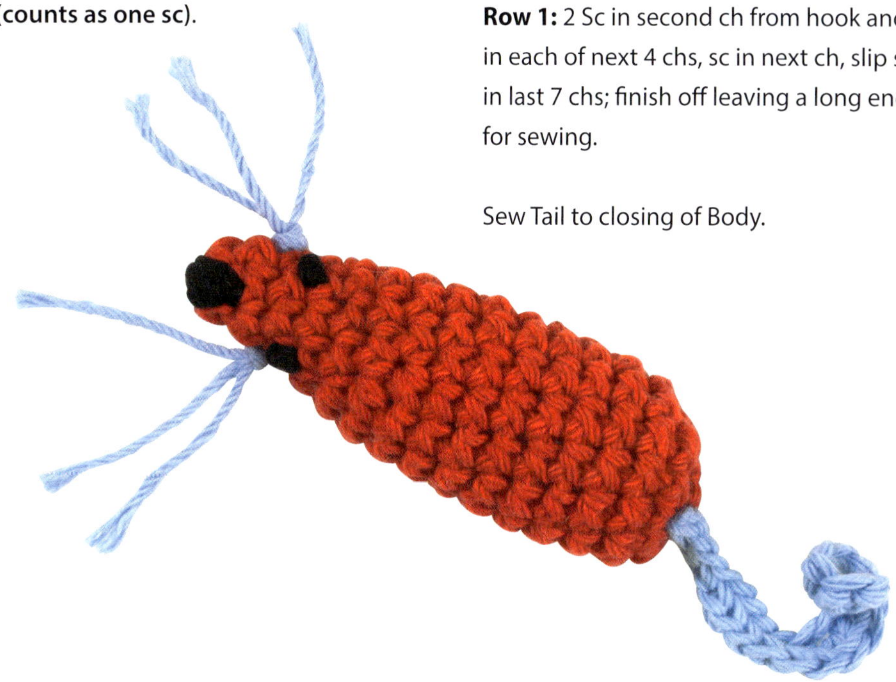

BODY

With Red, ch 4; join with slip st to form a ring.

Rnd 1 (Right side)**:** 5 Sc in ring; do **not** join, place marker to indicate beginning of rnd *(see Markers, page 123)*.

Note: Loop a short piece of yarn around any stitch to mark Rnd 1 as **right** side.

Rnds 2-8: 2 Sc in next sc, sc in each sc around: 12 sc.

Rnds 9-14: Sc in each sc around.

Stuff Mouse firmly with polyester fiberfill.

Rnd 15: Sc2tog around; slip st in next st, finish off leaving a long end for sewing: 6 sts.

Thread yarn needle with long end and weave through remaining stitches on Rnd 15; gather **tightly** to close and secure end.

TAIL

With Blue, ch 14.

Row 1: 2 Sc in second ch from hook and in each of next 4 chs, sc in next ch, slip st in last 7 chs; finish off leaving a long end for sewing.

Sew Tail to closing of Body.

WHISKERS

Cut 3 strands of Blue, each 10" (25.5 cm) long.

Holding all 3 strands together, tie an overhand knot about 2" (5 cm) from one end. Insert the crochet hook all the way through Rnd 2 of the Body, hook strands on long side of the knot and pull through until the knot touches the Body. Tie another overhand knot so that it will rest tightly against the opposite side of the Body.

Trim the strands.

Using photo as a guide for placement and Black, work French knots for eyes ***(Fig. B)*** and satin stitch for nose ***(Fig. C)***.

Designs by Carolyn Christmas.

FRENCH KNOT

Bring needle up at 1. Wrap yarn around the needle the desired number of times and insert needle at 2, holding end of yarn with non-stitching fingers ***(Fig. B)***. Tighten knot; then pull needle through, holding yarn until it must be released.

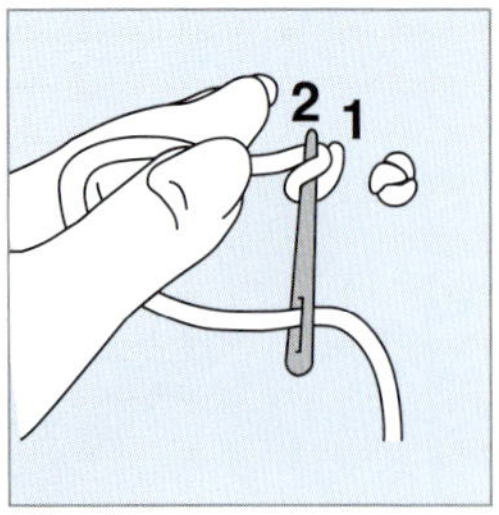

Fig. B

SATIN STITCH

Satin Stitch is a series of straight stitches that come out of and go into the same stitch. Come up at odd numbers and go down at even numbers ***(Fig. C)***.

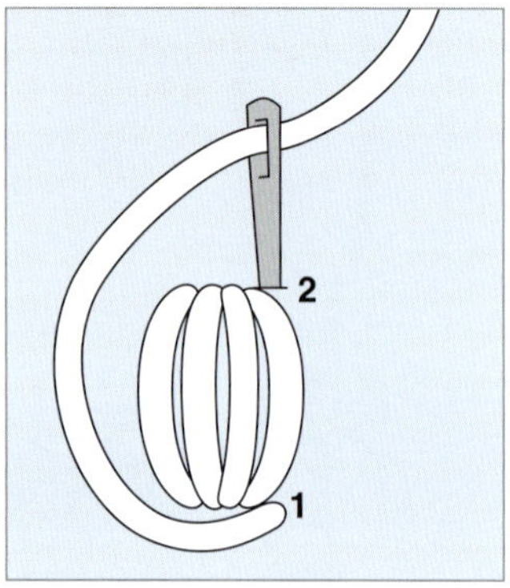

Fig. C

CREATIVITY

"..the power to connect the seemingly unconnected."

Crocheters will not only connect it, but will use a slip stitch to do so!

for storage in any room

Oval Baskets

EASY

SHOPPING LIST

Yarn (Medium Weight) MEDIUM 4
[2.8 ounces, 140 yards
(80 grams, 128 meters) per skein]:
- ☐ Main Color - 1{2-4} skein(s)
- ☐ Contrasting Color - 1 skein

Crochet Hook
- ☐ Size H (5 mm)
  or size needed for gauge

SIZE INFORMATION

Size: Small{Medium-Large}

Finished Bottom:
6{8¼-12}" long x 4{4¾-6}" wide/
15{21-30.5} cm x 10{12-15} cm

Finished Height:
4¾{6-8¾}"/12{15-22} cm
(before edging or folding on Large)

Size Note: We have printed the instructions for the sizes in different colors to make it easier for you to find:
- Size Small in Blue
- Size Medium in Pink
- Size Large in Green

Instructions in Black apply to all sizes.

GAUGE INFORMATION

13 sc and 12 rows/rnds = 4" (10 cm)

Gauge Swatch: 4" (10 cm) square

Holding 2 strands of Main Color together, ch 14.

Row 1: Sc in second ch from hook and in each ch across: 13 sc.

Rows 2-12: Ch 1, turn; sc in each sc across.

Finish off.

BOTTOM

Holding 2 strands of Main Color together, ch 9{15-22}.

Rnd 1 (Right side)**:** Sc in second ch from hook and in each ch across to last ch, 3 sc in last ch; working in free loops of beginning ch ***(Fig. 5b, page 124)***, sc in next 6{12-19} chs, 2 sc in next ch; join with slip st to first sc: 18{30-44} sc.

Note: Loop a short piece of yarn around any stitch to mark Rnd 1 as **right** side.

Rnd 2: Ch 1, sc in same st as joining and in next 7{13-20} sc, 3 sc in next sc, sc in next 8{14-21} sc, 3 sc in last sc; join with slip st to first sc: 22{34-48} sc.

Rnd 3: Ch 1, sc in same st as joining and in next 7{13-20} sc, 2 sc in next sc, sc in next sc, 2 sc in next sc, sc in next 8{14-21} sc, 2 sc in next sc, sc in next sc, 2 sc in last sc; join with slip st to first sc: 26{38-52} sc.

Rnd 4: Ch 1, sc in same st as joining and in next 6{12-19} sc, 2 sc in next sc, (sc in next sc, 2 sc in next sc) 3 times, sc in next 6{12-19} sc, 2 sc in next sc, (sc in next sc, 2 sc in next sc) twice, sc in last sc and in same sc as first sc; join with slip st to first sc: 34{46-60} sc.

Rnd 5: Ch 1, sc in same st as joining and in next 7{13-20} sc, 2 sc in next sc, sc in next 7 sc, 2 sc in next sc, sc in next 8{14-21} sc, 2 sc in next sc, sc in next 7 sc, 2 sc in last sc; join with slip st to first sc: 38{50-64} sc.

SIZE SMALL ONLY

Rnd 6: Ch 1, sc in same st as joining and in next 8 sc, 2 sc in next sc, (sc in next 3 sc, 2 sc in next sc) twice, sc in next 10 sc, 2 sc in next sc, (sc in next 3 sc, 2 sc in next sc) twice, sc in last sc: join with slip st to Back Loop Only of first sc ***(Fig. 4, page 124)***: 44 sc.

SIZES MEDIUM & LARGE ONLY

Rnd 6: Ch 1, sc in same st as joining and in next {14-21} sc, 2 sc in next sc, (sc in next 3 sc, 2 sc in next sc) twice, sc in next {16-23} sc, 2 sc in next sc, (sc in next 3 sc, 2 sc in next sc) twice, sc in last sc; join with slip st to first sc: {56-70} sc.

SIZE MEDIUM ONLY

Rnd 7: Ch 1, sc in same st as joining and in next 15 sc, 2 sc in next sc, sc in next 9 sc, 2 sc in next sc, sc in next 17 sc, 2 sc in next sc, sc in next 9 sc, 2 sc in next sc, sc in last sc; join with slip st to Back Loop Only of first sc ***(Fig. 4, page 124)***: 60 sc.

"What's that yarn for?"
"Baskets."
"What are the baskets for?"
"To hold more yarn."
Silly questions.

SIZE LARGE ONLY

Rnd 7: Ch 1, sc in same st as joining and in next 22 sc, 2 sc in next sc, (sc in next 4 sc, 2 sc in next sc) twice, sc in next 24 sc, 2 sc in next sc, (sc in next 4 sc, 2 sc in next sc) twice, sc in last sc; join with slip st to first sc: 76 sc.

Rnd 8: Ch 1, sc in same st as joining and in next 23 sc, 2 sc in next sc, sc in next 3 sc, 2 sc in next sc, sc in next 2 sc, 2 sc in next sc, sc in next 3 sc, 2 sc in next sc, sc in next 26 sc, 2 sc in next sc, sc in next 3 sc, 2 sc in next sc, sc in next 2 sc, 2 sc in next sc, sc in next 3 sc, 2 sc in next sc, sc in last 2 sc; join with slip st to first sc: 84 sc.

Rnd 9: Ch 1, sc in same st as joining and in each sc around; join with slip st to Back Loop Only of first sc *(Fig. 4, page 124)*.

SIDES (All Sizes)

Rnd 1: Ch 1, sc in Back Loop Only of same st as joining and each sc around; join with slip st to **both** loops of first sc: 44{60-84} sc.

Rnds 2 thru 14{18-26}: Ch 1, sc in both loops of same st as joining and each sc around; join with slip st to first sc.

Finish off.

TRIM

Add one of the following trims to any size basket.

FRINGE

Holding 3 strands of Contrasting Color together, each 10" (25.5 cm) long, add fringe in every other sc on last rnd *(Figs. 15a & b, page 126)*.

SHELL EDGING

Rnd 1: With **right** side facing, join one strand of Contrasting Color with sc in any sc on last rnd *(see Joining With Sc, page 123)*; sc in each sc around; join with slip st to first sc: 44{60-84} sc.

Rnd 2: Ch 1, sc in same st as joining, skip next sc, 5 dc in next sc, skip next sc, ★ sc in next sc, skip next sc, 5 dc in next sc, skip next sc; repeat from ★ around; join with slip st to first sc, finish off.

LSC EDGING

Rnd 1: With **right** side facing, join 2 strands of Contrasting Color with sc in any sc on last rnd *(see Joining With Sc, page 123)*; sc in next 2 sc, work LSC in sc one rnd **below** next sc *(Fig. 11, page 125)*, ★ sc in next 3 sc, work LSC in sc one rnd **below** next sc; repeat from ★ around; join with slip st to first sc, finish off.

Designs by Marly Bird.

Puff Stitch Basket

BASIC

Finished Size:
9½" long x 7" wide x 3¾" deep
(24 cm x 18 cm x 9.5 cm)

SHOPPING LIST

Yarn (Medium Weight) MEDIUM 4
[3.5 ounces, 153 yards
(100 grams, 140 meters) per skein]:
- ☐ Coral - 1 skein
- ☐ Blue - 1 skein
- ☐ Cream - 1 skein

Crochet Hook
- ☐ Size G (4 mm)
  or size needed for gauge

GAUGE INFORMATION

In Bottom pattern,
17 sc and 19 rows = 4" (10 cm)
Gauge Swatch: 6½" wide x 4" high
(16.5 cm x 10 cm)
Work same as Bottom through Row 19, do **not** finish off: 28 sc.

STITCH GUIDE

PUFF STITCH ***(abbreviated Puff St)*** (uses one sc)
★ YO, insert hook in sc indicated, YO and pull up loop; repeat from ★ 2 times **more** (7 loops on hook), YO and draw through all 7 loops on hook, ch 1 to close.

FRONT POST DOUBLE CROCHET ***(abbreviated FPdc)***
Working in **front** of previous rnds, YO, insert hook from **front** to **back** around post of st indicated ***(Fig. 6, page 124)***, YO and pull up a loop (3 loops on hook), (YO and draw through 2 loops on hook) twice. Skip sc behind FPdc.

DOUBLE CROCHET 2 TOGETHER ***(abbreviated dc2tog)*** (uses next 2 sts)
★ YO, insert hook in **next** st, YO and pull up a loop, YO and draw through 2 loops on hook; repeat from ★ once **more**, YO and draw through all 3 loops on hook **(counts as one dc)**.

DOUBLE CROCHET 3 TOGETHER ***(abbreviated dc3tog)*** (uses next 3 sts)
★ YO, insert hook in **next** st, YO and pull up a loop, YO and draw through 2 loops on hook; repeat from ★ 2 times **more**, YO and draw through all 4 loops on hook **(counts as one dc)**.

BOTTOM

With Coral, ch 29.

Row 1: Sc in second ch from hook and in each across: 28 sc.

Row 2 (Right side)**:** Ch 1, turn; sc in each sc across.

Note: Loop a short piece of yarn around any stitch to mark Row 2 as **right** side.

Rows 3-42: Ch 1, turn; sc in each sc across.

Do **not** finish off.

TRIM

Ch 1, do **not** turn; † skip first row, sc in end of next row and in each row across to last row, skip last row †; working in free loops of beginning ch ***(Fig. 5b, page 124)***, 3 sc in ch at base of first sc on Row 1, sc in next 26 chs, 3 sc in last ch; repeat from † to † once; 3 sc in first sc on Row 42, sc in next 26 sc, 3 sc in last sc; join with slip st to first sc, finish off: 144 sc.

SIDES

Rnd 1: With **right** side facing and working in Back Loops Only ***(Fig. 4, page 124)***, join Cream with slip st in center sc of of last 3-sc group on Trim, ch 2 **(counts as first hdc, now and throughout)**, sc in next 42 sc, hdc in next sc, sc in next 28 sc, hdc in next sc, sc in next 42 sc, hdc in next sc, sc in next 28 sc; join with slip st to first hdc: 140 sc and 4 corner hdc.

Rnd 2: Ch 2, working in Back Loops Only, sc in each sc across to next corner hdc, (hdc in corner hdc, sc in each sc across to next corner hdc) around; join with slip st to **both** loops of first hdc changing to Blue ***(Fig. 7a, page 124)***, cut Cream.

Rnd 3: Ch 3 **(counts as first hdc plus ch 1)**, skip next sc, work Puff St in next sc, ★ † (ch 1, skip next sc, work Puff St in next sc) across to next corner hdc †, hdc in corner hdc; repeat from ★ 2 times **more**, then repeat from † to † across; join with slip st to first hdc changing to Cream, cut Blue: 74 sts and 70 ch-1 sps.

Rnd 4: Ch 2, working **around** next ch ***(Fig. 8, page 125)***, dc in skipped sc on Rnd 2, sc in top of next Puff St, (working **around** next ch, dc in skipped sc on Rnd 2, sc in top of next Puff St) across to next corner hdc, ★ hdc in corner hdc, (working **around** next ch, dc in skipped sc **below** ch, sc in top of next Puff St) across to next corner hdc; repeat from ★ around; join with slip st to Back Loop Only of first hdc: 144 sts.

Rnd 5: Ch 2, working in Back Loops Only, sc in each st across to next corner hdc, (hdc in corner hdc, sc in each sc across to next corner hdc) around; join with slip st to **both** loops of first hdc.

Rnd 6: Ch 2, (work FPdc around next dc on Rnd 4, sc in next sc) across to next corner hdc, ★ hdc in corner hdc, (work FPdc around next dc on Rnd 4, sc in next sc) across to next corner hdc; repeat from ★ around; join with slip st to first hdc.

Rnd 7: Ch 2, sc in each st across to next corner hdc, (hdc in corner hdc, sc in each st across to next corner hdc) around; join with slip st to first hdc.

Rnd 8: Ch 2, (sc in next sc, work FPdc around next sc on Rnd 6) across to next corner hdc, ★ hdc in corner hdc, (sc in next sc, work FPdc around next sc on Rnd 6) across to next corner hdc; repeat from ★ around; join with slip st to first hdc.

Rnd 9: Repeat Rnd 7.

Rnd 10: Ch 2, (work FPdc around next sc on Rnd 8, sc in next sc) across to next corner hdc, ★ hdc in corner hdc, (work FPdc around next sc on Rnd 8, sc in next sc) across to next corner hdc; repeat from ★ around; join with slip st to first hdc.

Rnd 11: Ch 2, † [skip next 2 sts, (sc, ch 2, sc) in next st] 13 times, ch 1, skip next 3 sts, hdc in next corner hdc, [skip next 2 sts, (sc, ch 2, sc) in next st] 9 times, skip next sc †, hdc in next corner hdc; repeat from † to † once; join with slip st to first hdc: 92 sts and 46 sps.

Rnd 12: Ch 2, skip next sc, † sc in next ch-2 sp, [skip next 2 sc, 7 dc in next ch-2 sp, skip next 2 sc, sc in next ch-2 sp] 6 times, skip next sc and next ch-1 sp, hdc in next corner hdc, skip next sc, sc in next ch-2 sp, [skip next 2 sc, 7 dc in next ch-2 sp, skip next 2 sc, sc in next ch-2 sp] 4 times, skip next sc †, hdc in next corner hdc, repeat from † to † once; join with slip st to first hdc: 168 sts.

Rnd 13: Ch 2, † dc2tog, hdc in next dc, sc in next 3 dc, hdc in next dc, (dc3tog, hdc in next dc, sc in next 3 dc, hdc in next dc) 5 times, (dc2tog, hdc in next st) twice, sc in next 3 dc, hdc in next dc, (dc3tog, hdc in next dc, sc in next 3 dc, hdc in next dc) 3 times, dc2tog †, hdc in next hdc; repeat from † to † once; join with slip st to first hdc: 128 sts.

Rnd 14: Ch 2, † sc in next 37 sts, hdc in next corner hdc, sc in next 25 sts †, hdc in next corner hdc; repeat from † to † once; join with slip st to first hdc changing to Blue, do **not** cut Cream.

Rnd 15: Ch 2, hdc in next st and in each st around; join with slip st to first hdc changing to Cream, cut Blue.

Rnd 16: Ch 2, working in horizontal bar of hdc ***(Fig. 9, page 125)***, hdc in next hdc and each hdc around; join with slip st to first hdc, finish off.

Rnd 17: With **right** side facing, join Coral with slip st in first hdc; slip st in each st around; join with slip st to first slip st, finish off.

Design by Kristi Simpson.

Striped Basket

EASY

Finished Size:
31" circumference x 7" high
(78.5 cm x 18 cm)

SHOPPING LIST

Yarn (Super Bulky Weight) SUPER BULKY 6
[8 ounces, 149 yards
(227 grams, 136 meters) per skein]:
- ☐ Gray - 1 skein
- ☐ White - 1 skein
- ☐ Purple - 1 skein

Crochet Hook
- ☐ Size M/N (9 mm)
  or size needed for gauge

GAUGE INFORMATION

9 sts = 4" (10 cm)

Gauge Swatch: 3" (7.5 cm) diameter
Work same as Bottom through Rnd 2: 20 sc.

BOTTOM

Rnd 1 (Right side)**:** With Gray, ch 4, 9 dc in fourth ch from hook **(3 skipped chs count as first dc)**; join with slip st to first dc: 10 dc.

Note: Loop a short piece of yarn around any stitch to mark Rnd 1 as **right** side.

Rnd 2: Ch 1, 2 sc in each dc around; join with slip st to first sc: 20 sc.

Rnd 3: Ch 3 **(counts as first dc, now and throughout)**, 2 dc in next sc, (dc in next sc, 2 dc in next sc) around; join with slip st to first dc: 30 dc.

Rnd 4: Ch 1, sc in same st as joining and in next dc, 2 sc in next dc, (sc in next 2 dc, 2 sc in next dc) around; join with slip st to first sc: 40 sc.

Rnd 5: Ch 3, dc in next 2 sc, 2 dc in next sc, (dc in next 3 sc, 2 dc in next sc) around; join with slip st to first dc: 50 dc.

Rnd 6: Ch 1, sc in same st as joining and in next 3 dc, 2 sc in next dc, (sc in next 4 dc, 2 sc in next dc) around; join with slip st to first sc: 60 sc.

Rnd 7: Ch 3, dc in next 4 sc, 2 dc in next sc, (dc in next 5 sc, 2 dc in next sc) around; join with slip st to first dc, do **not** finish off: 70 dc.

SIDES

Rnd 1: Ch 1, hdc in Back Loop Only of each dc around *(**Fig. 4, page 124**)*; join with slip st to first hdc.

Rnds 2 and 3: Ch 1, hdc in both loops of each hdc around; join with slip st to first hdc.

Finish off.

Rnd 4: With **right** side facing and working in both loops, join White with hdc in same st as joining *(**see Joining With Hdc, page 123**)*; hdc in next hdc and in each hdc around; join with slip st to first hdc, finish off.

Rnd 5: With **right** side facing and working in Back Loops Only, join Purple with hdc in same st as joining; hdc in next hdc and in each hdc around; join with slip st to first hdc, finish off.

Rnd 6: With Gray, repeat Rnd 5.

Rnds 7-12: Repeat Rnds 4-6 twice; do **not** finish off at end of Rnd 12.

Rnd 13: Ch 1, working in both loops, hdc in same st as joining and in next 12 hdc, ch 12 (handle), skip next 10 hdc, hdc in next 25 hdc, ch 12, skip next 10 hdc, hdc in last 12 hdc; join with slip st to first hdc: 50 hdc and 24 chs.

Rnd 14: Ch 1, hdc in same st as joining and in next 12 hdc, 12 hdc in next ch-12 sp, hdc in next 25 hdc, 12 hdc in next ch-12 sp, hdc in last 12 hdc; join with slip st to first hdc, finish off.

Design by Kristi Simpson.

for decoration and fun

Exuberant Embellishments

EASY

Finished Size: 27" wide x 28" long (68.5 cm x 71 cm)

SHOPPING LIST

Yarn

(Super Bulky Weight) SUPER BULKY 6
[7 ounces, 22 yards
(200 grams, 20 meters) per skein]:
☐ Color A - 3 skeins
[1.75 ounces, 27 yards
(50 grams, 25 meters) per skein]:
☐ Color B - 1 ball
(Jumbo Weight) JUMBO 7
[3.5 ounces, 55 yards
(100 grams, 50 meters) per skein]:
☐ Color C - 2 skeins
(Fine Weight) FINE 2
[1.75 ounces, 202 yards
(50 grams, 185 meters) per skein]:
☐ Color D - 1 skein
(Light Weight) LIGHT 3
[16 feet (5 meters) per card]:
☐ Color E - 2 cards

Crochet Hooks

☐ Size N/P (10 mm) **and**
☐ Size S (19 mm)
or sizes needed for gauge

Additional Supplies

☐ Round wooden dowel - ½" diameter x 27" long (1.25 cm x 68.5 cm)
☐ Wood stain (optional for dowel)
☐ Tapestry needle

GAUGE INFORMATION

With larger size hook,
4 sc and 3 rows = 4" (10 cm)
Gauge Swatch: 4" (10 cm)
With larger size hook and Color A, ch 5.
Row 1: Sc in second ch from hook and in each ch across: 4 sc.
Rows 2 and 3: Ch 1, turn; sc in each sc across.
Finish off.

STITCH GUIDE

TREBLE CROCHET ***(abbreviated tr)***
YO twice, insert hook in st indicated, YO and pull up a loop (4 loops on hook), (YO and draw through 2 loops on hook) 3 times.

BODY

With smaller size hook and holding one strand **each** of Color D and Color C together, ch 33.

Row 1 (Right side)**:** Dc in fourth ch from hook and in each ch across **(3 skipped chs count as first dc)**: 31 dc.

Note: Loop a short piece of yarn around any stitch to mark Row 1 as **right** side.

Row 2: Ch 4 **(counts as first dc plus ch 1)**, turn; skip first 2 dc, dc in next dc, ★ ch 1, skip next dc, dc in next dc; repeat from ★ across; finish off: 16 dc and 15 ch-1 sps.

The Body splits after Row 2 and is worked one side at a time. The First Side is worked with bulkier yarn with fewer rows than the Second Side, which is worked with lighter weight yarn.

FIRST SIDE

Row 1: With **right** side facing and larger size hook, skip first dc and join Color A with sc in next ch-1 sp ***(see Joining With Sc, page 123)***; (ch 1, sc in next ch-1 sp) 4 times, skip next ch-1 sp, (ch 1, sc in next ch-1 sp) 5 times, leave remaining 9 sts unworked: 10 sc and 9 ch-1 sps.

Row 2: Ch 2 **(counts as first sc plus ch 1, now and throughout)**, turn; skip next ch-1 sp, sc in next sc, ★ ch 1, skip next ch-1 sp, sc in next sc; repeat from ★ across.

Row 3: Ch 2, turn; skip next ch-1 sp, sc in next sc, ★ ch 1, skip next ch-1 sp, sc in next sc; repeat from ★ across to last 3 sc, leave remaining sts unworked: 7 sc and 6 ch-1 sps.

Row 4: Repeat Row 2.

Row 5: Ch 2, turn; skip next ch-1 sp, sc in next sc, ★ ch 1, skip next ch-1 sp, sc in next sc; repeat from ★ 2 times **more**, leave remaining sts unworked: 5 sc and 4 ch-1 sps.

Row 6: Repeat Row 2; finish off.

SECOND SIDE

Row 1: With **right** side facing, smaller size hook, and holding one strand **each** of Color C and Color B together, join yarn with sc in first unworked dc on Row 2 of Body; (sc in next ch-1 sp and in next dc) across: 9 sc.

Row 2: Ch 1, turn; sc in first 9 sc, slip st in side of sc on Row 1 of First Side.

Row 3: Ch 1, turn; sc in each sc across.

Row 4: Ch 1, turn; sc in first 9 sc, slip st in side of sc on Row 2 of First Side.

Row 5: Ch 1, turn; sc in each sc across.

Row 6: Ch 1, turn; sc in first 9 sc, 2 sc in first sc on Row 2 of First Side, (2 sc in next ch-1 sp and in next sc) twice, sc in next ch-1 sp, slip st in side of sc on Row 3 of First Side: 20 sc.

Row 7: Ch 1, turn; sc in each sc across; cut Color B, add one strand of Color D.

Row 8: Ch 1, turn; sc in each sc across, sc in first sc on Row 4 of First Side and in next ch-1 sp, sc in next sc and in next ch-1 sp, slip st in side of sc on Row 5 of First Side: 24 sc.

Row 9: Ch 1, turn; sc in each sc across; do **not** finish off.

TOP

Row 1: Ch 1, turn; sc in each sc across, skip first sc on Row 6 of First Side, (sc in next ch-1 sp and in next sc) across: 32 sc.

Row 2: Ch 4 **(counts as first tr, now and throughout)**, turn; tr in next sc and in each sc across.

Row 3: Ch 1, turn; sc in first 8 tr; cut Color D, add one strand of Color B, sc in each tr across.

Row 4: Ch 3 **(counts as first dc)**, turn; dc in next 15 sc, finish off; using larger size hook and Color A, (sc in next sc, skip next sc) 7 times, sc in last 2 sc: 25 sts.

Row 5: Ch 2 **(counts as first hdc)**, turn; hdc in next 8 sc and in next dc, (skip next dc, hdc in next dc) 6 times, skip next dc, hdc in last 2 dc: 18 hdc.

Row 6: Ch 4, turn; tr in next hdc and in each hdc across.

Row 7: Ch 4, turn; tr in next tr and in each tr across; finish off.

FINISHING

POM-POM

(Make 3 with Color D and one with Color C)

Make each pom-pom 3½" (9 cm) ***(Figs. 13a-c, page 126)***.

TASSEL

Make 3 with Color D, each 7" (18 cm) long
Make 2 with Color C, each 6" (15 cm) long
Make 1 with Color B, 5½" (14 cm) long

Make tassels ***(Figs. 14a & b, page 126)***.

Using photo as a guide for placement, attach pom-poms and tassels to Body.

FRINGE

Cut 7 strands of Color A, each 20" (51 cm) long.

Using photo as a guide for placement, working in free loops of beginning ch ***(Fig. 5b, page 124)***, and using one strand, add fringe evenly spaced across bottom edge ***(Figs. 15a & b, page 127)***.

ATTACH DOWEL

Thread tapestry needle with double strand of Color E. With **right** side facing, sew overhand through Row 7 of Top and around the dowel; secure ends.

Design by Sharon H. Silverman.

Mandala

EASY

Finished Size:
10" (25.5 cm) diameter

SHOPPING LIST

Yarn (Medium Weight) MEDIUM 4
[3.5 ounces, 186 yards
(100 grams, 170 meters) per skein]:
- ☐ Aqua - 1 skein
- ☐ White - 1 skein
- ☐ Pink - 1 skein
- ☐ Rose - 1 skein
- ☐ Orange - 1 skein

Crochet Hook
- ☐ Size G (4 mm)
  or size needed for gauge

Additional Supplies
- ☐ 10" (25.5 cm) diameter metal ring

GAUGE INFORMATION

Gauge Swatch: $4^5/_8$" (11.75 cm) diameter
Work same as Center through Rnd 6:
48 dc, 16 chs, and 8 sc.

STITCH GUIDE

TREBLE CROCHET *(abbreviated tr)*
YO twice, insert hook in st indicated, YO and pull up a loop (4 loops on hook), (YO and draw through 2 loops on hook) 3 times.

DOUBLE TREBLE CROCHET *(abbreviated dtr)*
YO 3 times, insert hook in st indicated, YO and pull up a loop (5 loops on hook), (YO and draw through 2 loops on hook) 4 times.

FRONT POST SINGLE CROCHET *(abbreviated FPsc)*
Insert hook from **front** to **back** around post of st indicated ***(Fig. 6, page 124)***, YO and pull up a loop, YO and draw through both loops on hook.

FRONT POST DOUBLE CROCHET *(abbreviated FPdc)*
YO, insert hook from **front** to **back** around post of st indicated ***(Fig. 6, page 124)***, YO and pull up a loop (3 loops on hook), (YO and draw through 2 loops on hook) twice.

FRONT POST TREBLE CROCHET *(abbreviated FPtr)*
YO twice, insert hook from **front** to **back** around st indicated ***(Fig. 6, page 124)***, YO and pull up a loop (4 loops on hook), (YO and draw through 2 loops on hook) 3 times.

FRONT POST DOUBLE TREBLE CROCHET *(abbreviated FPdtr)*
YO 3 times, insert hook from **front** to **back** around st indicated ***(Fig. 6, page 124)***, YO and pull up a loop (5 loops on hook), (YO and draw through 2 loops on hook) 4 times.

PUFF STITCH *(abbreviated Puff St)*
(uses one sc)
★ YO, insert hook in st indicated, YO and pull up a loop; repeat from ★ 2 times **more** (7 loops on hook), YO and draw through all 7 loops on hook.

PICOT
Ch 2, slip st in top of dtr just made.

CENTER

Rnd 1 (Right side)**:** With Aqua, ch 2, work 8 hdc in second ch from hook; join with slip st to first hdc.

Note: Loop a short piece of yarn around any stitch to mark Rnd 1 as **right** side.

Rnd 2: Ch 2 **(does not count as a st, now and throughout)**, working in horizontal bar of each hdc ***(Fig. 9, page 125)***, 2 hdc in same st as joining and each hdc around; join with slip st to first hdc, finish off: 16 hdc.

Work Center with **right** side facing throughout.

Rnd 3: Join White with slip st in any hdc; (ch 4, dtr, work Picot, dtr, ch 4, slip st) in same st, ★ slip st in next 2 hdc, (ch 4, dtr, work Picot, dtr, ch 4, slip st) in same st as last slip st made; repeat from ★ around to last hdc, slip st in last hdc, place marker in last hdc worked into for st placement; join with slip st to joining slip st, finish off: 8 Picots.

Rnd 4: Join Orange with slip st in last Picot made on Rnd 3; ch 6, working **around** next slip st *(Fig. 8, page 125)*, slip st in marked hdc, remove marker, ch 6, ★ slip st in next Picot, ch 6, slip st **around** next slip st and in hdc on Rnd 2, ch 6; repeat from ★ around; join with slip st to joining slip st, finish off.

Rnd 5: Join Rose with slip st in Back Loop Only *(Fig. 4, page 124)* of same st as joining; ch 1, 2 sc in same st, slip st in top loops *(Fig. 3, page 124)* of first 4 chs of next ch-6 and last 4 chs of next ch-6, ★ 3 sc in Back Loop Only of next slip st, slip st in top loops of first 4 chs of next ch-6 and last 4 chs of next ch-6; repeat from ★ around, sc in same slip st as first sc; join with slip st to first sc, finish off: 64 slip sts and 24 sc.

Work in Back Loops Only through Rnd 14.

Rnd 6: Join Aqua with sc in same st as joining *(see Joining With Sc, page 123)*; ch 1, skip next sc and next 3 slip sts, 3 dc in each of next 2 slip sts, ch 1, skip next 3 slip sts and next sc, ★ sc in next sc, ch 1, skip next sc and next 3 slip sts, 3 dc in each of next 2 slip sts, ch 1, skip next 3 slip sts and next sc; repeat from ★ around; join with slip st to first sc changing to White *(Fig. 7a, page 124)*, cut Aqua: 48 dc, 16 chs, and 8 sc.

Rnd 7: Ch 1, sc in same st as joining and in next 7 sts, 2 sc in next ch, (sc in next 8 sts, 2 sc in next ch) around; join with slip st to first sc changing to Pink, cut White: 80 sc.

Rnd 8: Ch 1, sc in each sc around; join with slip st to first sc, finish off.

Rnd 9: Skip first 3 sc and join Rose with sc in next sc; sc in next 4 sc, work FPtr around Back Loop Only of center sc on Rnd 5, ch 3, working **below** FPtr just made, work FPtr around same loop, skip next 5 sc from last sc made, ★ sc in next 5 sc, work FPtr around Back Loop Only of next center sc on Rnd 5, ch 3, working **below** FPtr just made, work FPtr around same loop, skip next 5 sc from last sc made; repeat from ★ around; join with slip st to first sc changing to White, cut Rose: 40 sc, 16 FPtr, and 8 ch-3 sps.

Rnd 10: Ch 1, sc in same st as joining and in next 4 sc, ★ † sc in next FPtr, working in **front** of next ch-3 ***(Fig. 8, page 125)***, (tr, ch 1, tr) in free loop of sc on Rnd 6 ***(Fig. 5a, page 125)***, sc in next FPtr on Rnd 9 †, sc in next 5 sc; repeat from ★ 6 times **more**, then repeat from † to † once; join with slip st to first sc, finish off: 56 sc, 16 tr, and 8 ch-1 sps.

Rnd 11: Join Orange with sc in last tr; ★ † sc in next 7 sc and in next tr, working in **front** of next ch-1 and **between** tr, 2 dc in same loop as tr †, sc in next tr; repeat from ★ 6 times **more**, then repeat from † to † once; join with slip st to first sc, finish off: 72 sc and 16 dc.

Rnd 12: Join White with sc in same st as joining; sc in next 8 sc, work FPdc around next 2 tr on Rnd 10, skip next 2 dc, ★ sc in next 9 sc, work FPdc around next 2 tr on Rnd 10, skip next 2 dc; repeat from ★ around; join with slip st to first sc changing to Rose, cut White.

Rnd 13: Ch 1, 2 sc in same st, sc in next 8 sc, work FPdtr around next 2 FPtr on Rnd 9, skip next 2 FPdc on Rnd 12, ★ 2 sc in next sc, sc in next 8 sc, work FPdtr around next 2 FPtr on Rnd 9, skip next 2 FPdc on Rnd 12; repeat from ★ around; join with slip st to first sc, finish off: 80 sc and 16 FPdtr.

Rnd 14: Skip first sc and join Aqua with slip st in next sc; ch 2, work Puff St in same st, ch 2, ★ skip next st, work Puff St in next st, ch 2; repeat from ★ around to last sc, skip last sc; join with slip st to top of first Puff St, finish off: 48 Puff Sts and 48 ch-2 sps.

Rnd 15: Join White with slip st in both loops at top of first Puff St, working in **front** of next ch-2, dc in Back Loop Only of skipped sc **below**, ★ slip st in **both** loops at top of next Puff St, working in **front** of next ch-2, dc in Back Loop Only of skipped st **below**; repeat from ★ around; join with slip st to first slip st, finish off: 48 dc and 48 slip sts.

Rnd 16: Working in Back Loops Only, join Rose with sc in first dc; sc in next 10 sts, work FPtr around **both** posts of 2 FPdtr on Rnd 13, ★ sc in next 12 sts, work FPtr around **both** posts of 2 FPdtr on Rnd 13; repeat from ★ around to last slip st, work FPtr around **both** posts of last 2 FPdtr on Rnd 13, sc in last slip st; join with slip st to **both** loops of first sc, finish off: 104 sts.

Joining Rnd: Join Rose with sc around metal ring; work 25 sc, with **right** side of Center facing, work FPdc around any FPtr on Rnd 16, ★ work 26 sc around metal ring, work FPsc around next FPtr on Rnd 15; repeat from ★ around; join with slip st to first sc, finish off.

FINISHING

TASSEL (Make 3)

Make two Rose tassels and one Orange tassel, each 6" (15 cm) long, wrapping the yarn around the cardboard approximately 24 times ***(Figs. 14 & b, page 126)***. Tuck the long yarn ends at top of each tassel into the tassel. Trim the ends.

JOINING

Center Tassel: With **right** side facing, join Orange with slip st in FPdc on Joining Rnd; ch 8, slip st around top yarn end on Orange Tassel; finish off.

Side Tassel: With **right** side facing, join Rose with slip st in tenth sc **before** Center Tassel; ch 15, slip st around top yarn end on one Rose Tassel; finish off.

Last Tassel: With **right** side facing, join Rose with slip st in tenth sc **after** Center Tassel, ch 15, slip st around top yarn end on last Rose Tassel; finish off.

Hanger: With **wrong** side facing, skip 2 FPsc from Center Tassel and join Orange with slip st around next FPsc; ch 80; skip next FPsc, slip st around next FPsc; finish off.

Design by Kristi Simpson.

Banner

EASY

Finished Size: Approximately 3¾" (9.5 cm) high

SHOPPING LIST

Yarn (Lace Weight) 0 LACE

- ☐ Color A (Yellow) - 75 yards (68.5 meters)
- ☐ Color B (Orange) - 75 yards (68.5 meters)
- ☐ Color C (Green) - 95 yards (87 meters)

Note: It takes a total of 25 yards (23 meters) for **each** triangle

Steel Crochet Hook

- ☐ Size 6 (1.8 mm) **or** size needed for gauge
- ☐ Basket

GAUGE INFORMATION

Gauge Swatch: 2½" (6.25 cm) high

Work same as Triangle through Rnd 4: 18 sps.

STITCH GUIDE

CLUSTER (uses one st)

★ YO, insert hook in st indicated, YO and pull up a loop, YO and draw through 2 loops on hook; repeat from ★ 2 times **more**, YO and draw through all 4 loops on hook.

TRIANGLE (Make 9 **total**)

Work in the following color sequence:

Rnd(s)	Make 3	Make 3	Make 3
1	Color A	Color B	Color C
2-4	Color B	Color C	Color A
5 & 6	Color C	Color A	Color B
7	Color A	Color B	Color C

Rnd 1 (Right side)**:** With color indicated, ch 4, work (Cluster, ch 3, slip st) in fourth ch from hook, [ch 3, (work Cluster, ch 3, slip st) in same ch] twice **(3-petal group made)**, ★ ch 8, work (Cluster, ch 3, slip st) in fourth ch from hook, [ch 3, (work Cluster, ch 3, slip st) in same ch] twice **(3-petal group made)**; repeat from ★ once **more**, ch 4; join with slip st to same ch as first Cluster, finish off: three 3-petal groups.

Note: Loop a short piece of yarn around any stitch to mark Rnd 1 as **right** side.

Rnd 2: With **right** side facing, join next color with sc in first ch-3 sp of any center petal ***(see Joining With Sc, page 123)***; ch 3, skip next Cluster, sc in next ch-3 sp, ch 5, sc in next Cluster, ch 3, sc in first Cluster on next 3-petal group, ch 5, ★ sc in first ch-3 sp of center petal, ch 3, skip next Cluster, sc in next ch-3 sp, ch 5, sc in next Cluster, ch 3, sc in first Cluster on next 3-petal group, ch 5; repeat from ★ once **more**; join with slip st to first sc: 12 sps.

Rnd 3: Slip st in next ch-3 sp, ch 3 **(counts as first dc, now and throughout)**, (2 dc, ch 3, 3 dc) in same sp, ch 1, 3 dc in next ch-5 sp, ch 1, (dc, ch 3, dc) in next ch-3 sp, ch 1, 3 dc in next ch-5 sp, ch 1, ★ (3 dc, ch 3, 3 dc) in next ch-3 sp, ch 1, 3 dc in next ch-5 sp, ch 1, (dc, ch 3, dc) in next ch-3 sp, ch 1, 3 dc in next ch-5 sp, ch 1; repeat from ★ once **more**; join with slip st to first dc: 42 dc and 18 sps.

Rnd 4: Slip st in next 2 dc and in next ch-3 sp, ch 3, (2 dc, ch 3, 3 dc) in same sp, ch 1, 3 dc in next ch-1 sp, ch 1, skip next ch-1 sp, (3 dc, ch 1) twice in next ch-3 sp, skip next ch-1 sp, 3 dc in next ch-1 sp, ch 1, ★ (3 dc, ch 3, 3 dc) in next ch-3 sp, ch 1, 3 dc in next ch-1 sp, ch 1, skip next ch-1 sp, (3 dc, ch 1) twice in next ch-3 sp,

skip next ch-1 sp, 3 dc in next ch-1 sp, ch 1; repeat from ★ once **more**; join with slip st to first dc, finish off: 18 sps.

Rnd 5: With **right** side facing, join next color with dc in next ch-3 sp after joining ***(see Joining With Dc, page 123)***; (2 dc, ch 3, 3 dc) in same sp, (ch 1, 3 dc in next ch-1 sp) twice, ch 3, sc in next ch-1 sp, ch 3, (3 dc in next ch-1 sp, ch 1) twice, ★ (3 dc, ch 3, 3 dc) in next ch-3 sp, (ch 1, 3 dc in next ch-1 sp) twice, ch 3, sc in next ch-1 sp, ch 3, (3 dc in next ch-1 sp, ch 1) twice; repeat from ★ once **more**; join with slip st to first dc: 57 sts and 21 sps.

Rnd 6: Slip st in next 2 dc and in next ch-3 sp, ch 3, (2 dc, ch 3, 3 dc) in same sp, ch 1, (3 dc in next sp, ch 1) 6 times, ★ (3 dc, ch 3, 3 dc) in next ch-3 sp, ch 1, (3 dc in next sp, ch 1) 6 times; repeat from ★ once **more**; join with slip st to first dc, finish off: 72 dc and 24 sps.

Rnd 7: With **right** side facing, join next color with sc in any ch-3 sp; sc in same sp and in next 3 dc, (sc in next ch-1 sp and in next 3 dc) 7 times, ★ 3 sc in next ch-3 sp, sc in next 3 dc, (sc in next ch-1 sp and in next 3 dc) 7 times; repeat from ★ once **more**, sc in same sp as first sc; join with slip st to first sc, finish off: 102 sc.

With desired color, make a chain to fit around basket plus 16" (40.5 cm) for ties. Slip st in second ch from hook and in each ch across; finish off.

Using photo as a guide, weave piece though spaces on one side of each triangle; tie around top edge of basket and make a tight knot to secure, spacing Triangles evenly; then tie in a bow.

Design by Darla Sims.

Wall Hanger

EASY

Finished Size: Fits a 4" (10 cm) pot

SHOPPING LIST

Yarn (Medium Weight Cotton) MEDIUM 4
[2.5 ounces, 120 yards
(70.9 grams, 109 meters) per skein]:
☐ 60 yards (55 meters)

Crochet Hook
☐ Size H (5 mm)
or size needed for gauge

Additional Supplies
☐ 3" (7.5 cm) metal ring

GAUGE INFORMATION

7 hdc = 2" (5 cm)
Gauge Swatch: 3½" (9 cm) diameter
Work same as Bottom through Rnd 5: 24 sc.

STITCH GUIDE

DOUBLE CROCHET 2 TOGETHER ***(abbreviated dc2tog)*** (uses next 2 sts)
★ YO, insert hook in **next** st, YO and pull up a loop, YO and draw through 2 loops on hook; repeat from ★ once **more**, YO and draw through all 3 loops on hook **(counts as one dc)**.

DOUBLE CROCHET 3 TOGETHER ***(abbreviated dc3tog)*** (uses next 3 sts)
★ YO, insert hook in **next** st, YO and pull up a loop, YO and draw through 2 loops on hook; repeat from ★ 2 times **more**, YO and draw through all 4 loops on hook **(counts as one dc)**.

PICOT
Ch 4, slip st in third ch from hook, ch 1.

BOTTOM

Ch 6; join with slip st to form a ring.

Rnd 1 (Right side)**:** Ch 1, 8 sc in ring; do **not** join, place marker to indicate beginning of rnd ***(see Markers, page 123)***.

Note: Loop a short piece of yarn around any stitch to mark Rnd 1 as **right** side.

Rnd 2: 2 Sc in in each sc around: 16 sc.

Rnd 3: (Sc in next sc, 2 sc in next sc) around: 24 sc.

Rnd 4: Sc in Back Loop Only of each sc around ***(Fig. 4, page 124)***.

Rnd 5: Sc in both loops of each sc around; do **not** finish off.

SIDES

Rnd 1: ★ Sc in next 2 sc, ch 9, hdc in third ch from hook and in each ch across (strip made), skip next sc; repeat from ★ around: 8 strips.

Rnd 2: Sc in next sc, slip st in next sc and in free loops of next 7 chs ***(Fig. 5b, page 124)***, slip st in space at end of strip, move marker to last slip st made for joining placement, ch 3, (slip st in sp at end of next strip, ch 3) around; join with slip st in Back Loop Only of marked slip st; remove marker: 24 chs.

Rnd 3 (Right side)**:** Ch 1, hdc in Back Loop Only of same st as joining, hdc in next 3 chs, ★ hdc in Back Loop Only of next slip st, hdc in next 3 chs; repeat from ★ around; join with slip st to Back Loop Only of first hdc: 32 hdc.

Rnd 4: Ch 1, sc in Back Loop Only of same st as joining and each hdc around; join with slip st to **both** loops of first sc, finish off.

BASE

Row 1: With **right** side facing, skip first 20 sc and join yarn with sc in next sc ***(see Joining With Sc, page 123)***; sc in next 20 sc, leave remaining 11 sc unworked: 21 sc.

Rows 2 and 3: Ch 2 (does **not** count as a st), turn; skip first st, dc2tog, dc in next st and in each st across to last 3 sts, dc3tog: 13 dc.

Row 4: Ch 1, turn; sc in first dc, ★ work Picot, skip next dc, sc in next dc; repeat from ★ across: 7 sc and 6 Picots.

Row 5: Ch 4 **(counts as first dc plus ch 1)**, turn; slip st in next Picot, ch 1, (slip st in next Picot, ch 1) across, dc in last sc.

Row 6: Ch 1, turn; sc in first dc, ★ work Picot, working **around** next slip st, sc in Picot one row **below**; repeat from ★ across to last ch-1 sp, sc in last ch-1 sp, leave last dc unworked: 8 sc and 6 Picots.

Rows 7-10: Repeat Rows 5 and 6 twice; at end of Row 10, place marker in first Picot for st placement: 8 sc and 6 Picots.

Finish off.

RING

Rnd 1: Join yarn with sc around metal ring; sc evenly around until ring is full; join with slip st to Back Loop Only of first sc.

Rnd 2: Ch 1, sc in Back Loop Only of each sc around; join with slip st to **both** loops of first sc.

Joining: Ch 4, turn; with **right** side of Base facing, slip st in marked Picot, remove marker, ch 4, skip next sc on **Ring**, slip st in next sc, ★ ch 4, slip st in next Picot on **Base**, ch 4, skip next sc on **Ring**, slip st in next sc; repeat from ★ 4 times **more**, ch 4, skip next sc on Base, slip st in last sc; finish off.

Design by Sarah J. Green.

'We make a living by what we get, but we make a life by what we give.' - Winston Churchill
If you give a crocheted gift, it is wonderful; but to teach someone to crochet... priceless.

General Instructions

ABBREVIATIONS

BPhdc	Back Post half double crochet(s)
BPsc	Back Post single crochet(s)
BPtr	Back Post treble crochet(s)
CC	Contrasting Color
ch(s)	chain(s)
cm	centimeters
dc	double crochet(s)
dc2tog	double crochet 2 together
dc3tog	double crochet 3 together
dtr	double treble crochet(s)
FPdc	Front Post double crochet(s)
FPdtr	Front Post double treble crochet(s)
FPhdc	Front Post half double crochet(s)
FPsc	Front Post single crochet(s)
FPtr	Front Post treble crochet(s)
hdc	half double crochet(s)
LSC	long single crochet(s)
MC	Main Color
mm	millimeters
Rnd(s)	Round(s)
sc	single crochet(s)
sc2tog	single crochet 2 together
sp(s)	space(s)
st(s)	stitch(es)
tr	treble crochet(s)
YO	yarn over

SYMBOLS & TERMS

★ — work instructions following ★ as many **more** times as indicated in addition to the first time.

† to † **or** ♥ to ♥ — work all instructions from first † to second † **or** first ♥ to second ♥ **as many** times as specified.

( ) or **[ ]** — work enclosed instructions **as many** times as specified by the number immediately following **or** work all enclosed instructions in the stitch or space indicated **or** contains explanatory remarks.

colon (:) — the number(s) given after a colon at the end of a row or round denote(s) the number of stitches and spaces you should have on that row or round.

Yarn Weight Symbol & Names	LACE 0	SUPER FINE 1	FINE 2	LIGHT 3	MEDIUM 4	BULKY 5	SUPER BULKY 6	JUMBO 7
Type of Yarns in Category	Fingering, size 10 crochet thread	Sock, Fingering, Baby	Sport, Baby	DK, Light Worsted	Worsted, Afghan, Aran	Chunky, Craft, Rug	Super Bulky, Roving	Jumbo, Roving
Crochet Gauge* Ranges in Single Crochet to 4" (10 cm)	32-42 sts**	21-32 sts	16-20 sts	12-17 sts	11-14 sts	8-11 sts	6-9 sts	5 sts and fewer
Advised Hook Size Range	Steel*** 6 to 8, Regular hook B-1	B-1 to E-4	E-4 to 7	7 to I-9	I-9 to K-10½	K-10½ to M/N-13	M/N-13 to Q	Q and larger

*GUIDELINES ONLY: The chart above reflects the most commonly used gauges and hook sizes for specific yarn categories.

** Lace weight yarns are usually crocheted with larger hooks to create lacy openwork patterns. Accordingly, a gauge range is difficult to determine. Always follow the gauge stated in your pattern.

*** Steel crochet hooks are sized differently from regular hooks–the higher the number, the smaller the hook, which is the reverse of regular hook sizing.

CROCHET TERMINOLOGY		
UNITED STATES		INTERNATIONAL
slip stitch (slip st)	=	single crochet (sc)
single crochet (sc)	=	double crochet (dc)
half double crochet (hdc)	=	half treble crochet (htr)
double crochet (dc)	=	treble crochet (tr)
treble crochet (tr)	=	double treble crochet (dtr)
double treble crochet (dtr)	=	triple treble crochet (ttr)
triple treble crochet (tr tr)	=	quadruple treble crochet (qtr)
skip	=	miss

BASIC	Projects using basic stitches. May include basic increases and decreases.
EASY	Projects may include simple stitch patterns, color work, and/or shaping.
INTERMEDIATE	Projects may include involved stitch patterns, color work, and/or shaping.
COMPLEX	Projects may include complex stitch patterns, color work, and/or shaping using a variety of techniques and stitches simultaneously.

GAUGE

Exact gauge is **essential** for proper size. Before beginning your project, make the sample swatch given in the individual instructions in the yarn and hook specified. After completing the swatch, measure it, counting your stitches and rows or rounds carefully. If your swatch is larger or smaller than specified, **make another, changing hook size to get the correct gauge**. Keep trying until you find the size hook that will give you the specified gauge.

MARKERS

Markers are used to help distinguish the beginning of each round being worked. Place a 2" (5 cm) scrap piece of yarn before the first stitch of each round, moving marker after each round is complete.

JOINING WITH SC

When instructed to join with sc, begin with a slip knot on hook. Insert hook in stitch or space indicated, YO and pull up a loop, YO and draw through both loops on hook.

JOINING WITH HDC

When instructed to join with hdc, begin with a slip knot on hook. YO, holding loop on hook, insert hook in stitch or space indicated, YO and pull up a loop (3 loops on hook), YO and draw through all 3 loops on hook.

JOINING WITH DC

When instructed to join with hdc, begin with a slip knot on hook. YO, holding loop on hook, insert hook in stitch or space indicated, YO and pull up a loop (3 loops on hook), (YO and draw through 2 loops on hook) twice.

ADJUSTABLE LOOP

Wind yarn around two fingers to form a ring ***(Fig. 1a)***.

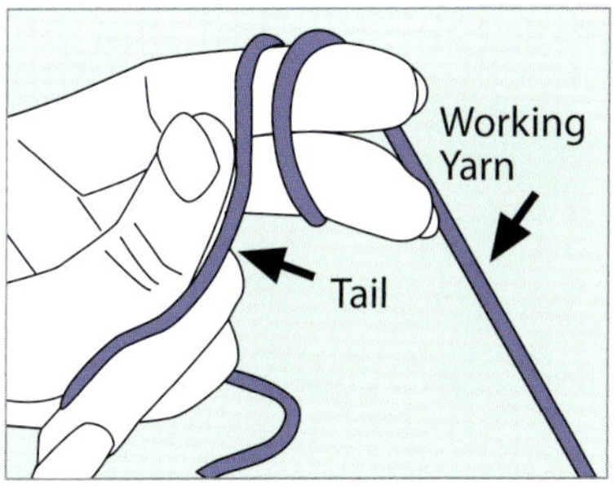

Fig. 1a

Slide yarn off fingers and grasp the strands at the top of the ring ***(Fig. 1b)***.

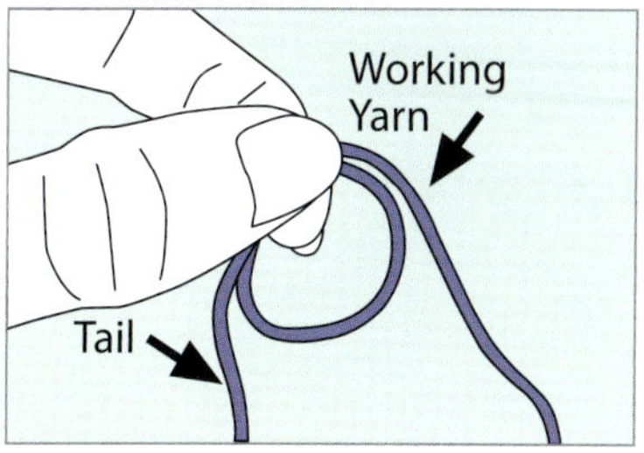

Fig. 1b

Insert hook from **front** to **back** into the ring, pull up a loop, YO and draw through loop on hook to lock ring ***(Fig. 1c)*** (st made does **not** count as part of beginning ch of first rnd).

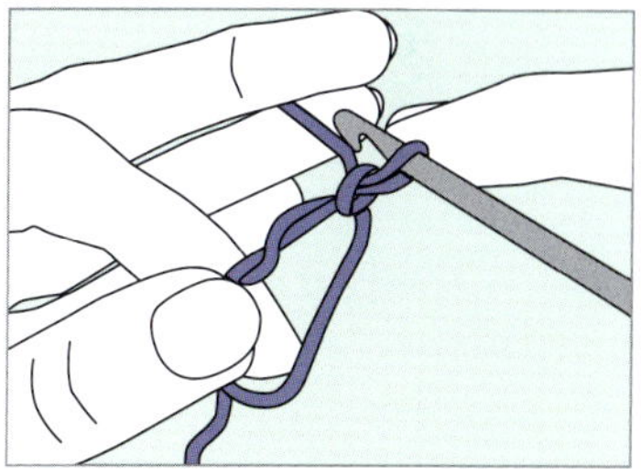

Fig. 1c

Working around **both** strands, follow instructions to work sts in the ring, then pull yarn tail to close ***(Fig. 1d)***.

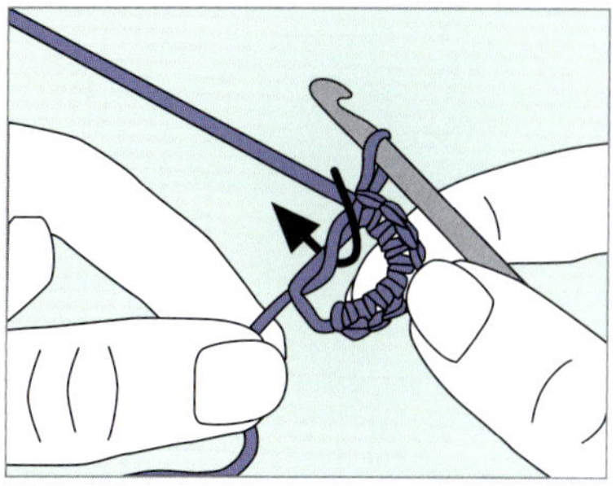

Fig. 1d

CROCHET HOOKS																	
U.S.	B-1	C-2	D-3	E-4	F-5	G-6	7	H-8	I-9	J-10	K-10½	L-11	M/N-13	N/P-15	P/Q	Q	S
Metric - mm	2.25	2.75	3.25	3.5	3.75	4	4.5	5	5.5	6	6.5	8	9	10	15	16	19

STEEL CROCHET HOOKS																
U.S.	00	0	1	2	3	4	5	6	7	8	9	10	11	12	13	14
Metric - mm	3.5	3.25	2.75	2.25	2.1	2.1	2.1	1.8	1.65	1.5	1.4	1.3	1.1	1	.85	.75

BACK RIDGE

Work only in loops indicated by arrows *(Fig. 2)*.

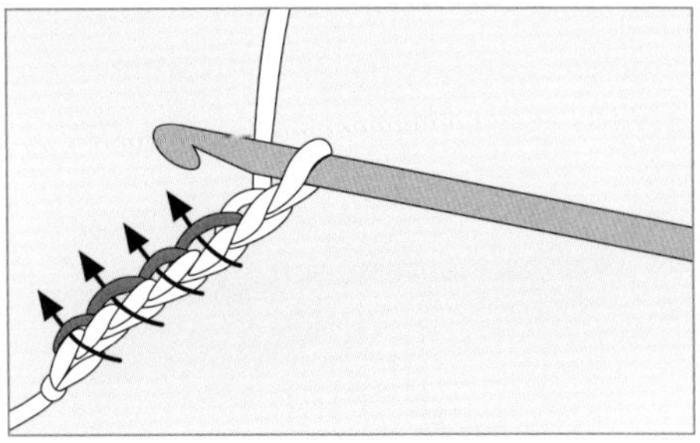

Fig. 2

TOP LOOPS

Work only in loops indicated by arrow *(Fig. 3)*.

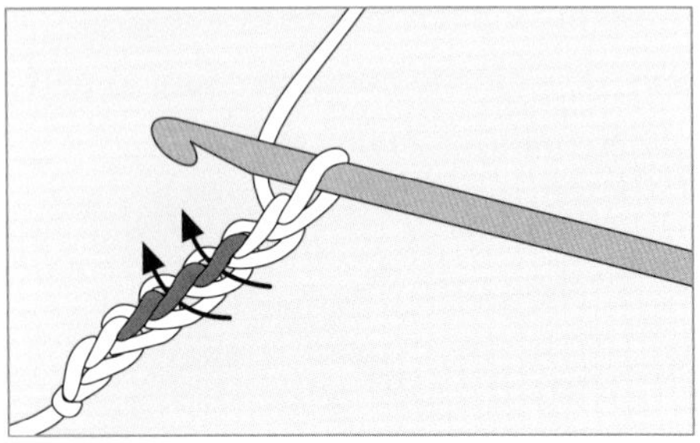

Fig. 3

BACK OR FRONT LOOP ONLY

Work only in loop(s) indicated by arrow *(Fig. 4)*.

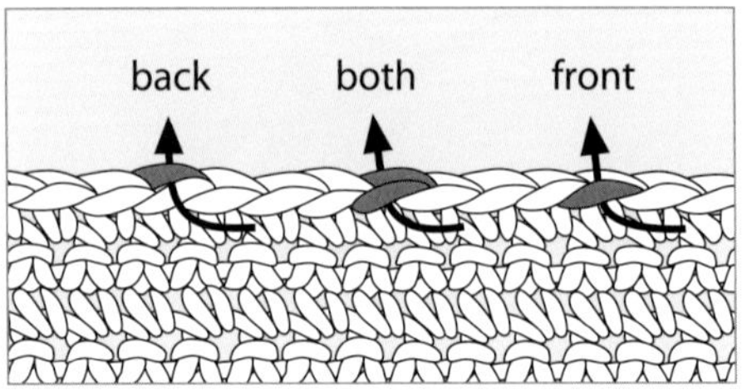

Fig. 4

FREE LOOPS

After working in Back or Front Loops Only on a row or round, there will be a ridge of unused loops. These are called the free loops. Later, when instructed to work in the free loops of the same row or round, work in these loops *(Fig. 5a)*. When instructed to work in free loops of a chain, work in loop indicated by arrow *(Fig. 5b)*.

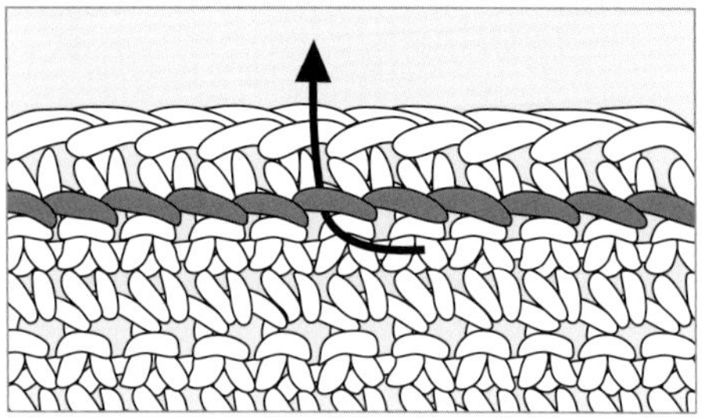

Fig. 5a

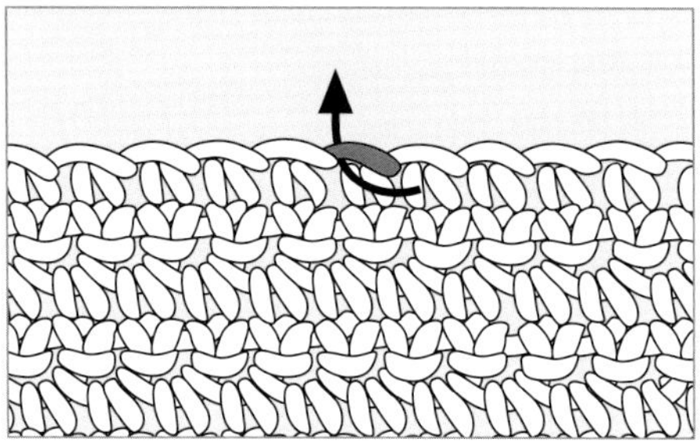

Fig. 5b

POST STITCH

Work around post of stitch indicated, inserting hook in direction of arrow *(Fig. 6)*.

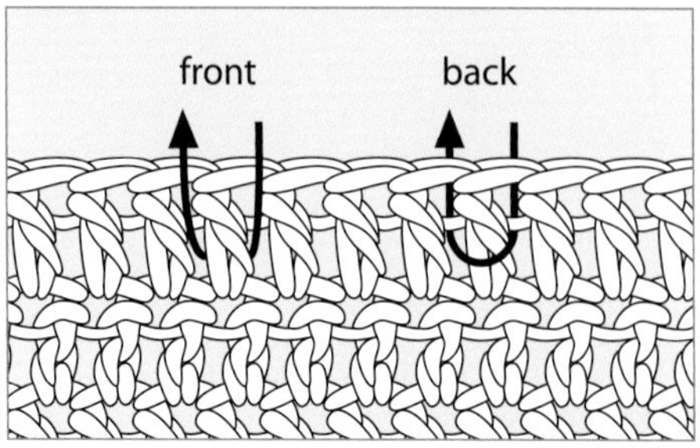

Fig. 6

CHANGING COLORS

To change colors while joining with a slip st, drop yarn, insert hook in first st, hook new yarn and draw through st and loop on hook ***(Fig. 7a)***.

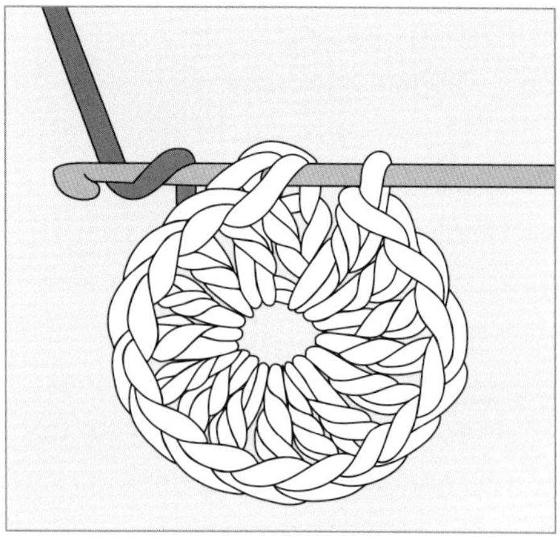

Fig. 7a

To change colors at the end of row, work last st to within one step of completion, drop yarn, with new yarn, YO and draw through remaining loops on hook ***(Figs. 7b-d)***. Do **not** cut old yarn unless instructed.

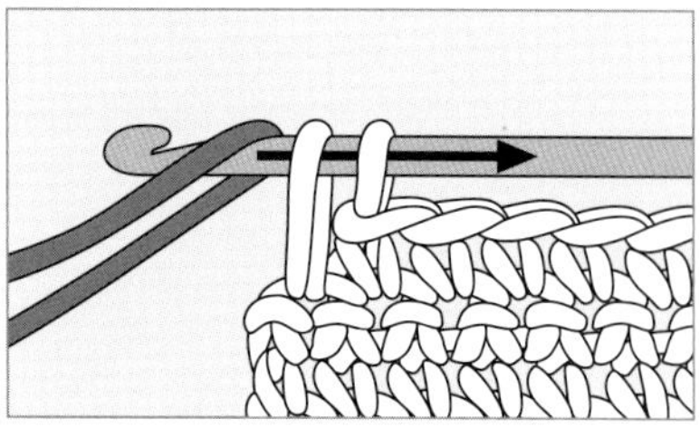

Fig. 7b

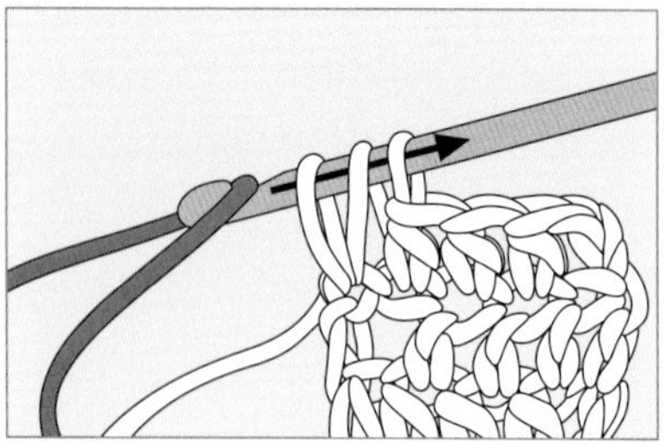

Fig. 7c

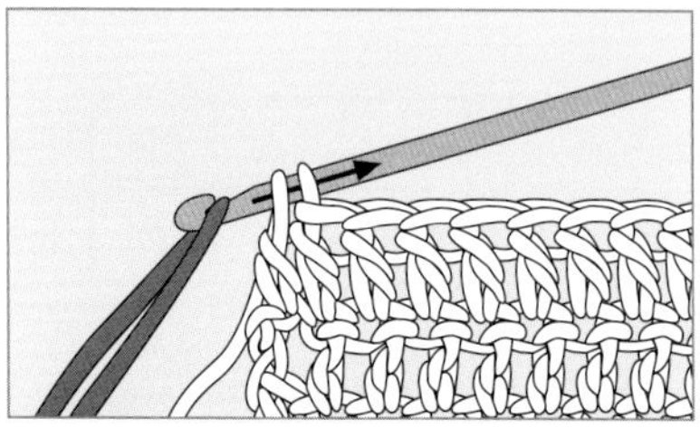

Fig. 7d

WORKING IN FRONT OF, AROUND, OR BEHIND A STITCH

Work in stitch or space indicated, inserting hook in direction of arrow *(Fig. 8)*.

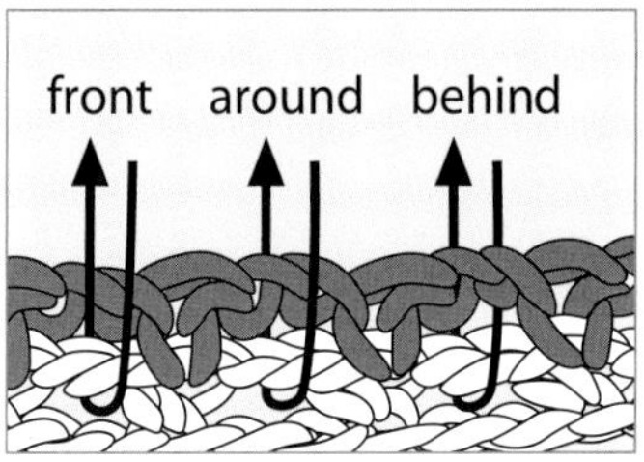

Fig. 8

WORKING IN HORIZONTAL BAR

When instructed to work in horizontal bar of hdc, work in loop indicated by arrow *(Fig. 9)*.

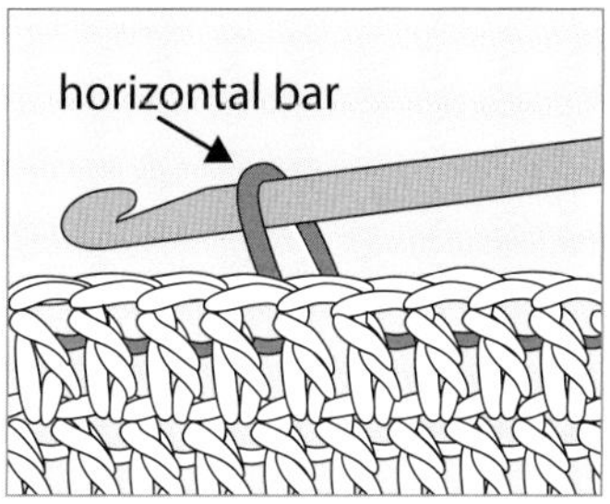

Fig. 9

REVERSE SINGLE CROCHET

(abbreviated reverse sc)

Working from **left** to **right**, ★ insert hook in st to right of hook ***(Fig. 10a)***, YO and draw through, under and to left of loop on hook (2 loops on hook) ***(Fig. 10b)***, YO and draw through both loops on hook ***(Fig. 10c)*** **(reverse sc made, *Fig. 10d*)**; repeat from ★ around.

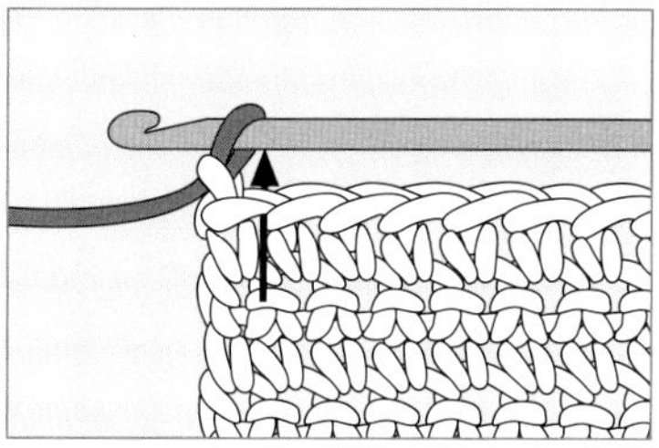

Fig. 10a

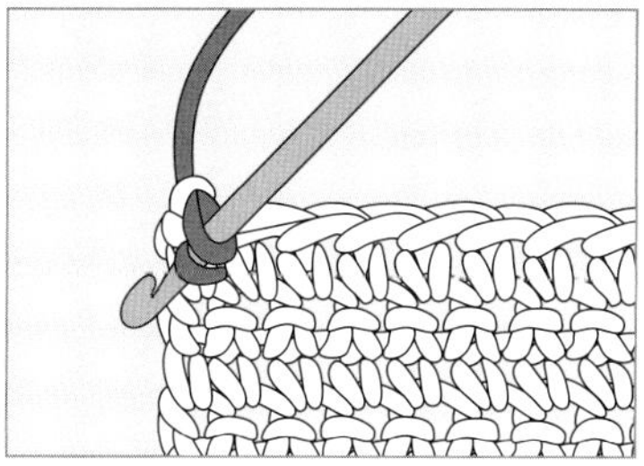

Fig. 10b

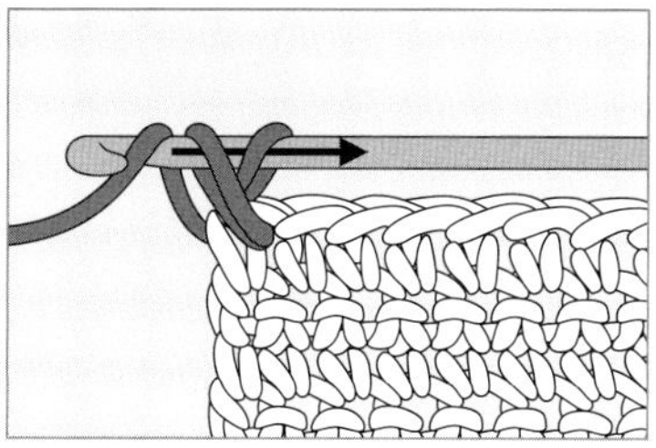

Fig. 10c

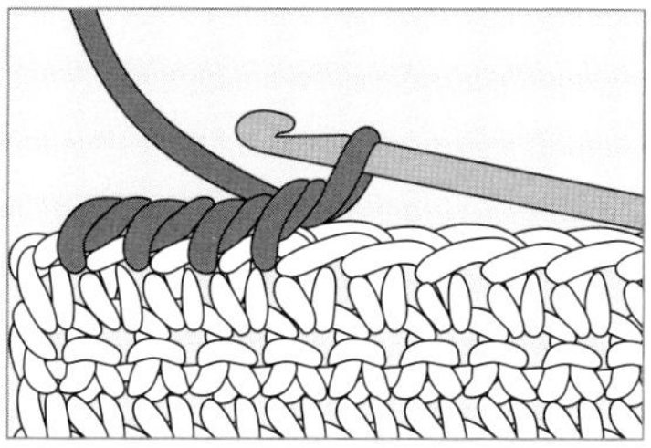

Fig. 10d

LONG SINGLE CROCHET

(abbreviated LSC)

Working **around** previous rnd, insert hook in sc indicated ***(Fig. 11)***, YO and pull up a loop even with last st made, YO and draw through both loops on hook.

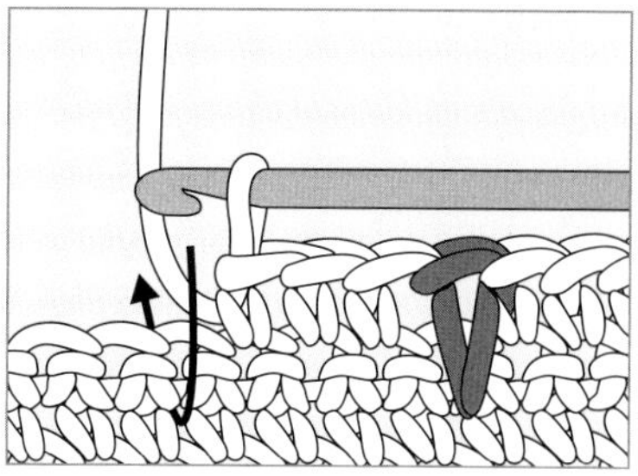

Fig. 11

WHIPSTITCH

Place two pieces with **wrong** sides together. Beginning in corner ch or st specified, sew through both pieces once to secure the beginning of the seam, leaving an ample yarn end to weave in later. Insert the needle from **front** to **back** through **both** loops on **both** pieces ***(Fig. 12a)*** **or** through **inside** loops only of each stitch on **both** pieces ***(Fig. 12b)***. Bring the needle around and insert it from **front** to **back** through next loops of both pieces. Continue in this manner across, keeping the sewing yarn fairly loose.

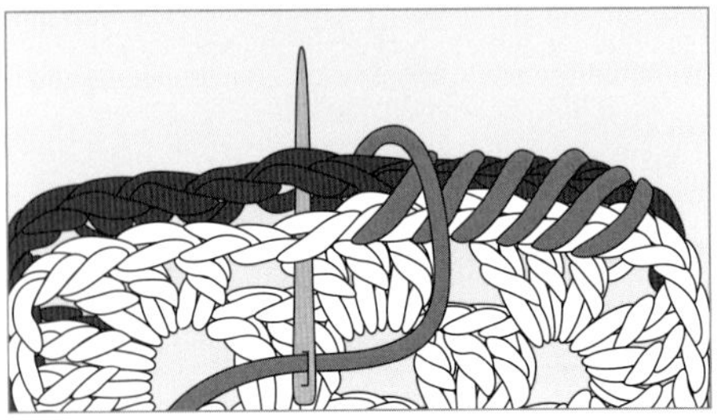

Fig. 12a

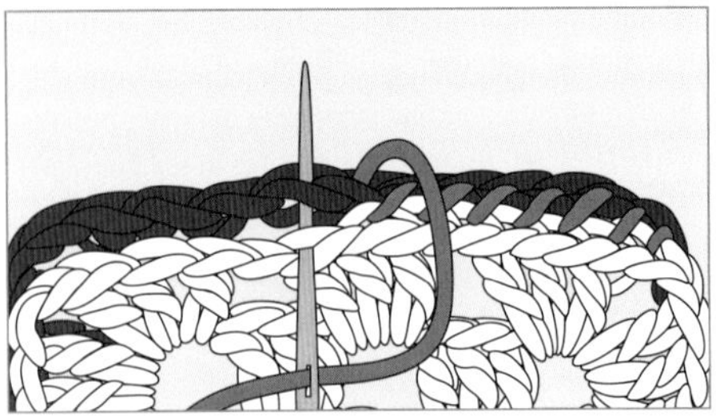

Fig. 12b

POM-POM

Cut a piece of cardboard 3" (7.5 cm) wide and as long as you want the diameter of your finished pom-pom to be.

Wind the yarn around the cardboard until it is approximately ½" (12 mm) thick in the middle ***(Fig. 13a)***.

Carefully slip the yarn off the cardboard and firmly tie an 18" (45.5 cm) length of yarn around the middle ***(Fig. 13b)***. Leave yarn ends long enough to attach the pom-pom. Cut the loops on both ends and trim the pom-pom into a smooth ball ***(Fig. 13c)***.

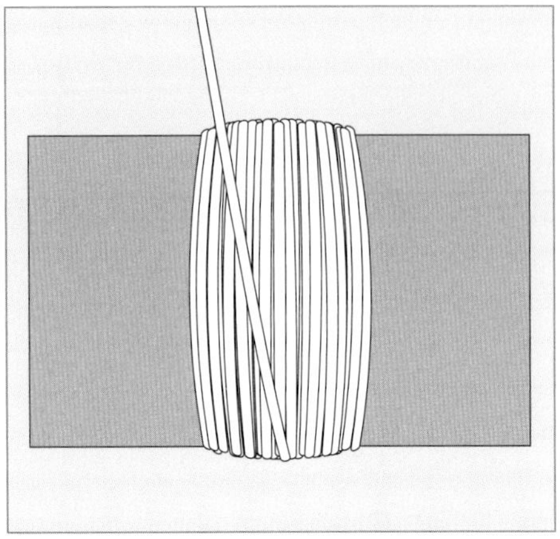

Fig. 13a

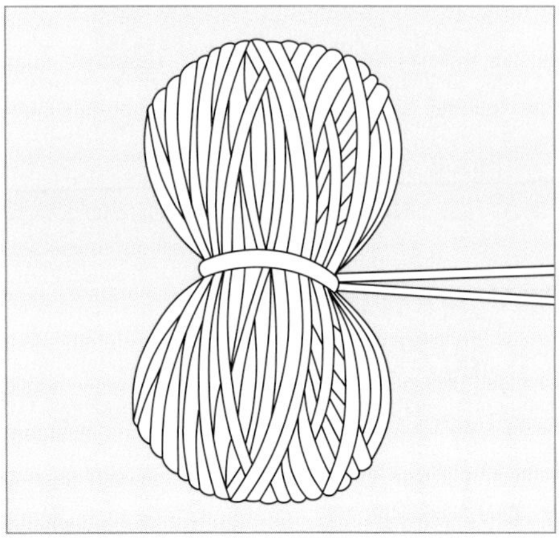

Fig. 13b

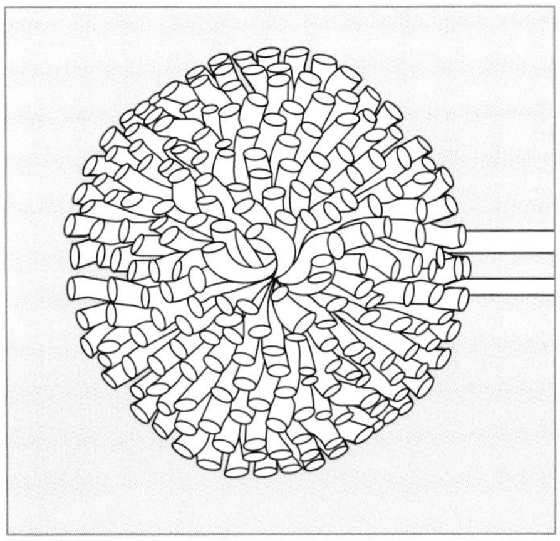

Fig. 13c

TASSEL

Cut a piece of cardboard 3" (7.5 cm) wide and as long as you want your finished tassel to be. Wind a double strand of yarn around the cardboard as many times as specified. Cut a 12" (30.5 cm) length of yarn and insert it under all of the strands at the top of the cardboard; pull up **tightly** and tie securely. Cut the yarn at the opposite end of the cardboard and then remove it ***(Fig. 14a)***. Cut a 6" (15 cm) length of yarn and wrap it **tightly** around the tassel twice, 1" (2.5 cm) below the top ***(Fig. 14b)***; tie securely. Trim the ends.

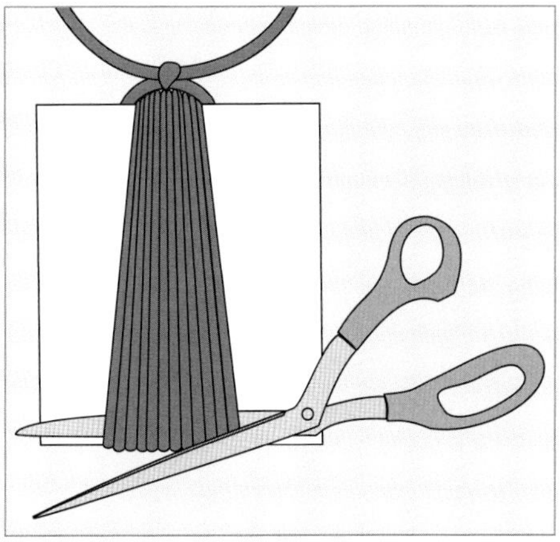

Fig. 14a

Fig. 14b

FRINGE

Cut a piece of cardboard 5" (12.5 cm) wide and ½" (12 mm) longer than you want your finished fringe to be. Wind the yarn **loosely** and **evenly** lengthwise around the cardboard until the card is filled, then cut across one end; repeat as needed.

Hold together as many strands as specified in individual instructions; fold in half.

With **wrong** side facing and using a crochet hook, draw the folded end up through a stitch and pull the loose ends through the folded end ***(Fig. 15a)***; draw the knot up **tightly** ***(Fig. 15b)***. Repeat, spacing as specified in individual instructions.

Lay flat on a hard surface and trim the ends.

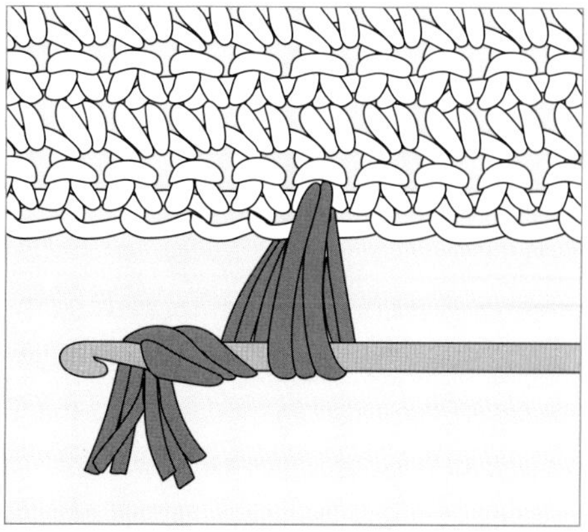

Fig. 15a

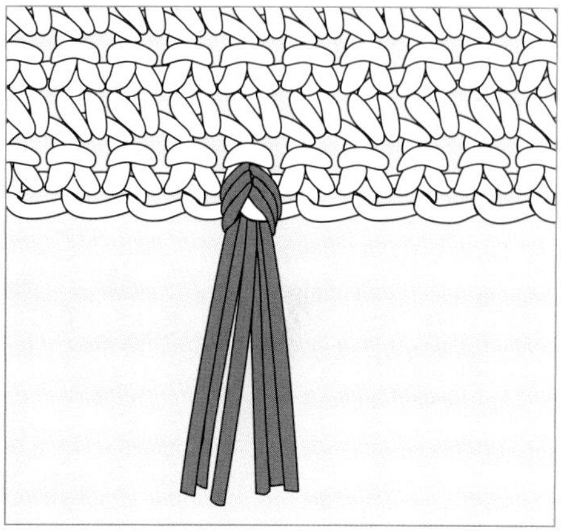

Fig. 15b

We have made every effort to ensure that these instructions are accurate and complete. We cannot, however, be responsible for human error, typographical mistakes, or variations in individual work.

Production Team: Instructional/ Technical Editor - Sarah J. Green; Senior Graphic Artist - Lora Puls; Graphic Artist - Maddy Ross; Photo Stylist - Lori Wenger; and Photographer - Jason Masters.

Library of Congress Control Number: 2019937415

Made in U.S.A.